MW00997086

Gharki Rasoi

Indian Home Cooking Made Simple

Purnima Gandhi

Dedicated to my mother,

Chandanben Muljibhai Mody,

who instilled in me a love of cooking.
Under her guidance I realized that cooking
and preparing meals for family and loved
ones can be an artform.

*During my first Diwali in the United States, when I was
missing all of the special traditional food my mother would
make for the family, all I had to do was mention it to her
and there was a parcel on my doorstep with all of my favorite
sweets. Each time she visited me in the United States, she
would make sure to pack all the necessary ingredients to
make my favorite dishes. Whenever I prepare an elaborate
meal, I can see her smiling down upon me.*

TABLE OF CONTENTS

FOREWARD

"Purnima is a remarkable individual, gifted instructor, and incredible cook. Her recipes are enticing, easy to follow, and unquestionably delicious. I should know, as I have used her recipes on countless occasions and always to rave reviews from my guests. Whether an experienced gourmand, a seasoned veteran of Indian Cuisine, or a newcomer looking to expand your palate, Purnima's recipes are a must have in any cooking repertoire!"

Patrick Newman,
Red Butte Garden, Programs Manager

"Through over twenty five years of friendship, I have enjoyed our conversations sitting around Purnima's kitchen counter as much as her cooking. When I think of her what immediately springs to mind are her creativity, willingness to try many different styles, and dishes, and innovatively modifying recipes for contemporary tastes and health needs. She is the most fearless and innovative cook I have encountered in my life and travels. She has brought her creativity to bear in modifying the cuisine for difficult to treat diabetic family members for years without sacrificing taste or flavors. She is also generous in sharing the techniques, methods, and details of recipes as an excellent teacher and a friend. The only thing better than trying out the recipes in this book is eating them. Enjoy!"

Rohit Patel
Retired Business Executive, Food & Wine Connoisseur

"I have had the privilege of knowing Purnima Gandhi for over 27 years, and during this time her culinary skills have always impressed me; as anything she made always was delicious and enjoyable to eat. She added to this talent when a family member was diagnosed with diabetes, and she learned all the nuances for a diabetes meal plan, and adapted her recipes to fit the nutrition recommendations for a diabetic person, which made her already healthy recipes even more nutritious. I recommend that any person interested in cooking tasty and healthy food for their family, get a copy of this culinary treasure and enjoy the journey of trying each recipe out with fun and health."

Karmeen Kulkarni, MS, RD, BC-ADM, CDE
Author, Nutrition consultant, and speaker

"Purnima introduced my family and me to the wild and wonderful world of Indian Cuisine. Together we pursued it across India from Calcutta to Delhi, Mumbai and beyond, only to discover that the best was to be found in Salt Lake City, Utah, created with love and care in Purnima's kitchen."

Jay Irwin, Retired Federal Judge

ACKNOWLEDGEMENTS

Creating a family cookbook has been an ongoing project for me. I have been teaching cooking classes and documenting recipes for more than 15 years. It would have been impossible for me to complete this book without the support and guidance of my family and friends. Special thanks to my daughters, Purvi and Priya. They spent countless hours editing, proofreading, designing, providing guidance and creative ideas, and taking pictures. I would like to thank my husband, Bipin, for being both proofreader and photographer, and my son-in-law Allen for being the final proofreader, to truly make this cookbook a family project. Special thanks to Rebecca Edwards, for helping me with my cooking classes and documenting them with pictures; to Karmeen Kulkarni, for providing encouragement and support as a friend, and guidance as a professional dietician; to Mridula Patel for her willingness to impart her knowledge of Indian ingredients and cooking methods; to my sister Pravina Kadakia for rekindling the family recipes on each of her visits; to Kalpana Madhok for introducing me to non-vegetarian cooking; Ashley Goodall for supplying the nutritional information for each recipe; and to Virginia Rainey for reviewing the recipes. Special thanks to Rohit Patel, Karmeen Kulkarni, Patrick Newman, and Jay Irwin for writing the foreword. Finally, I would like to thank everyone who had attended and participated in my cooking classes over the years. They have encouraged and inspired me to write this cookbook.

Purnima Gandhi
Salt Lake City, May 2013

INTRODUCTION

A common conception about Indian cooking is that it is very complicated, so in this book I have focused on simplifying the cooking process, recipes, and use of ingredients. The name "Gharki Rasoi" means "home-cooked meals," and the majority of the recipes in this book are taken from my everyday meals. Most of the ingredients are available in a regular grocery store, however some lentils and spices may require a trip to an Indian grocery store. Once you stock your pantry with basic Indian spices like mustard seeds, cumin, turmeric, red chili powder, coriander powder, and garam masala, you will be ready to go. I have provided nutritional information for most of the recipes and have also categorized them as vegan, vegetarian, and gluten free, to allow everyone to enjoy home-cooked Indian food, no matter their dietary preferences and restrictions.

Food was always at the center of every event in our family when I was growing up. I grew up helping my mom prepare the meals and was already cooking with her when I was eight or nine. My parents were the first in their families to migrate to Mumbai from the small village of Balasinor, located in the interior of Gujarat province. As was the custom in those days, whenever someone from the village needed to travel to Mumbai, they would come unannounced to our house any time night or day. And as the popular Indian tradition goes, a guest is never denied food and shelter since they are considered to represent God in one of their forms. In Sanskrit the saying goes:

> *Pitru Devo Bhava (Father is a form of God)*
> *Matru Devo Bhava (Mother is a form of God)*
> *Guru Devo Bhava (A teacher is also a form of God)*
> *Atithi Devo Bhava (God visits in the form of a guest)*

Atithi also means someone (a guest) who comes unexpected or without a fixed arrival date. Since feeding guests always fell on my mother's shoulders, she was glad to have my help in the kitchen.

Our family followed the "Vaishnav" tradition, which means we are followers of Lord Vishnu in the form of 'Srinathji'. Worshipping Srinathji in a Vaishnav family meant that the women of the family followed a strict sequence of events during the day, after waking up, and taking a bath. They had to wake Srinathji up by offering morning prayers after lighting an oil lamp, adorn him in proper garments and jewelry appropriate for the season, prepare a meal for him, send him off to tend the cows, and on his return feed him the night meal and put him to bed. No one ate before offering the food first to Srinathji and then the food was seen as a gift from God as Prasadam. In the Srimad Bhagavad Gita, this tradition is referred to as Bhakti Yoga, one of the four forms of Yoga.

There is a lot of richness and diversity in Indian cuisine rarely experienced outside India. It differs from state to state, province to province, and region to region. Even within a state or region the cuisine differs every few miles and within each village or family. Traditional food, along with India's history, dates back to more than five thousand years. India has been a melting pot of many cultures and traditions brought by travelers, invaders, and conquerors. Alexander the Great introduced Greek cooking and saffron from Persia, the Mughals brought dried fruits and some spices, and the Portuguese brought vinegar, as a souring agent for meats, into Goan cooking. Being part of the ancient trade routes by land and sea, India assimilated a lot of ingredients from all the cultures of the East and West.

The most interesting part of Indian cuisine is the variety of spices used in cooking. They add color, flavor, and taste. Indian food is spicy and flavorful. Spicy does not mean just hot, although that is the way most people outside India seem to identify it. Each family adapts the amount of chilies added to the food according to their tastes. To reduce heat, simply adjust the amount of chilies, but keep all other spices to maintain the flavor, taste, and presentation. Some basic spices used in everyday Indian cooking include asafetida, cumin, coriander, black pepper, turmeric, mustard seeds, fennel seeds, cinnamon, cardamom, cloves, and fenugreek. There are several common spice mixes like garam masala, tandoori masala, tikka masala, pavbhaji masala, sambhar masala, and chaat masala. They are used to enhance flavors of different dishes and represent major differences in regional cuisines.

As a child I grew up eating Gujarati food in the home, since my family roots are in Gujarat. Some of the popular dishes from Gujarat are Moothia, Vegetable Paratha (Thepla), Dhokla, and Daal Dhokli. I was introduced to the foods of other parts of India when eating out at restaurants with family and friends: North Indian (Punjabi, Kashmiri, and U.P.) food such as such as Chole, Bhatoora, Palak Paneer, and Naan, Tikka Masala, and Samosas; South Indian dishes such as Idli, Dosa, Sambhar, Wada, and Coconut Chutney; Bengali dishes like fish curries, Rasagulla, and Rasamalai; and Portuguese influenced dishes like Goan shrimp curry.

In this book I have tried to include the important dishes from most of the major regions of India, based on their popularity, taste and fit for this collection. I sincerely hope you enjoy reading, preparing, and eating the dishes as much as I have enjoyed writing about them.

INGREDIENTS & TOOLS

The ingredients of Indian cooking are surprisingly simple. There are a few staple spices - coriander, turmeric, chili powder, salt, cumin, mustard seeds, and fenugreek - along with a wide range of legumes/lentils with which you can make 80% of the recipes in this book. With the exception of a couple of vegetables, you should be able to make most anything in this book with ingredients you can find in a standard grocery store.

Below are most of the ingredients used in this book and a little bit about each and how it is used in Indian cooking. The list is generally sorted alphabetically by the English name in black (except for the daals since in the recipes the Indian names are used) with the Hindi name in red. The number next to some of the items corresponds to the photos in this chapter.

At the end of the list are descriptions and images of some of the special kitchen utensils that help with Indian cooking.

Almond *Badam*: This nut, along with the others in this list, is widely used in desserts and as a garnish.

Asafetida *Hing*: This pungent, almost unpleasant smelling spice is a resinous gum that is available in both solid and ground forms. It is used in very small amounts and typically sauteed in oil at the begining of preparation. When cooked, it develops a pleasant flavor and is known to help with digestion.

1 **Bay Leaves** *Tej Patta*: Fragrant leaves with pointed ends, bay leaves are used in their dried form. They are used to infuse flavor in rice and curries, and in their powdered form are found in spice blends. When using whole leaves, they are typically discarded after cooking.

6 **Bottle Gourd** *Doodhi/Lauki*: This squash has light green skin and white flesh. It is eaten when the vegetable is young.

3 **Cardamom** *Elaichi*: Native to India, it is one of the most used spices in regional cuisine. The pods can be used whole or the husk can be removed to release the seeds. They have a sharp initial bite that soon mellows into a delicate and refreshing fragrance.

8 **Carom Seeds** *Ajwain/Ajmo*: Pungent brown seeds which look like celery seeds. When crushed, they release a strong and aromatic fragrance.

Cashews *Kaju*: This nut is used in desserts such as kaju kutri. Cashews are native to Northeast Brazil and were brough to India by the Portugese in the 16th century.

5 *Chana, Kala* **Black Chana**: Dark brown in color, they are smaller than their chickpea cousins. This daal is used in its powdered from to thicken gravies and to add a nutty flavor.

9 *Chana Daal* **Bengal Gram Daal**: Skinned and split dried chickpeas, yellow in color.

7 **Chickpea/Garbanzo** *Chole*: One of the first cultivated legumes, chickpeas come in two varieties: kabuli, which are larger and light yellow (garbanzo), and desi, which are smaller and dark brown (kala chana). In Indian cooking chickpeas are used whole, split and roasted (daalia), and as a flour (besan).

Chickpea Flour *Besan*: This flour is a key ingredient in Indian cooking, forming the base for many batters, and as a thickening agent. In American cuisine, chickpea flour is often used as a substitute for wheat flours for those with gluten sensitivities.

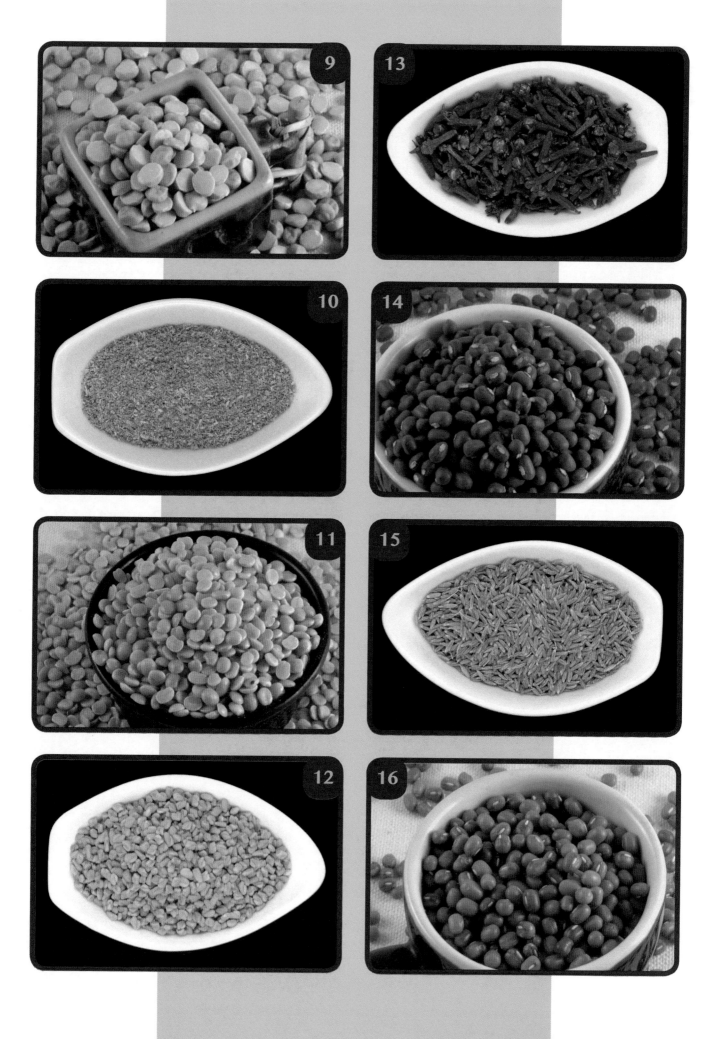

4 **Cilantro/Fresh Coriander** *Kothmir*: This leafy herb is used as a garnish and is the main ingredient in green chutney. About 5% of people have a genetic variation that makes cilantro taste like soap to them. In recipes garnished with cilantro, it may be replaced with flat leaf parsley. The tender stalks are full of flavor and they are chopped alongwith the leaves.

Cinnamon *Dalchini/Tuj*: In its whole form, cinnamon sticks are used to infuse flavor into rice and kadhi then discarded after cooking. Ground cinnamon is found in common spice blends such as garam masala.

13 **Cloves** *Luong/Lavang*: These dried unopened flower buds have a sharp and almost bitter taste. Used whole they infuse flavor into rice and vegetable dishes, while powdered they are found in spice blends.

10 **Coriander Powder** *Dhania Powder*: This spice is the ground seeds of the cilantro plant. It is often roasted in oil or ghee to release flavor and used as a thickening agent In gravies.

15 **Cumin** *Jeera*: Native to India and popular in regional cuisine, cumin may be used whole or ground. Whole cumin releases a strong aroma when fried in oil. Ground, roasted cumin lends a warm depth to dishes when pan fried and sprinkled as a garnish.

Curry Leaves *Kari Patta/Neem/Limdo*: Native to Southeast Asia, curry leaves can be used fresh or dried. They are often added to the oil at the beginning of the cooking process to fully infuse the dish with flavor, along with asafetida.

2 *Daalia* **Roasted Chana**: Roasted dried split chickpeas, used in chutneys or eaten whole as a snack.

Dates *Khajoor*: Dates have been a staple food for thousands of years in the Middle East and the Indus Valley and are believed to have originated in the area of present-day Iraq. They are used in Indian desserts and chutneys.

Dried Mango Powder *Amchoor*: Raw mangoes are sun dried and ground to a fine powder. The powder is then used as a souring agent and to flavor chutneys and sauces.

Fennel Seeds *Sounf/Vairali*: These oval, yellowish green seeds are sweet and add flavor to curries and rice. It is also common in many spice blends.

12 **Fenugreek Seeds** *Methi*: Pebble-like brown seeds, fenugreek is very bitter when raw, but mellows when cooked. Used sparingly when whole, and in spice blends when ground.

Fenugreek Greens *Methi Bhaji*: Fresh fenugreek leaves are used in vegetable parathas or moothia instead of spinach.

Garlic *Lasoon*: This is a standard ingredient, along with ginger and chilies, forming a fragrant base for many recipe sauces and gravies.

Ginger *Adarakh*: One of the most important ingredient in many dishes, ginger is used throughout Indian cuisine to add spiciness and warmth to dishes. It is most often finely chopped or grated.

Jaggery *Gur*: This standard Indian sweetener is the unrefined sugar from dates, sugarcane, or palm sap. It is minimally processed and has a very long shelf life. It typically comes in uneven chunks that are broken and added to recipes. Because it is not refined, it is one of the more healthy sugars.

Lemon & Lime *Limbu*: Lemon or lime juice is used in many Indian dishes to add tartness to vegetable or legume dishes.

Mint *Fudina*: Fresh mint is used in salted lassis and in making chutneys.

16 *Moong* **Whole Moong Beans**: This legume is native to the Indian Subcontinent. The outer skin is green, with a yellow flesh underneath. It is often served cooked whole.

17 *Moong Daal* **Split Moong Beans**: This legume is the green moong bean split and skinned, to reveal the yellow flesh.

18 **Mustard Seeds** *Rai/Sarson*: Indian cuisine uses the dark variety of these seeds. They have a sharp, pungent flavor which mellows after being sauteed in hot oil. It is used in seasoning lentils and vegetables.

20 **Nutmeg** *Jaiphal*: It has a rich fragrance and a sweet, warm flavor. It is used in desserts and various spice blends such as tea masala and birayani masala.

Okra (Ladyfingers) *Bhindi*: This green vegetable grows in tropical and warm temperate regions. It is high in fiber, vitamin C, folates, and antioxidants. It is also used in Middle Eastern, European, and Caribbean cuisine.

Onion *Kaanda/pyaaj*: Common red and yellow onions are widespread in indian cuisine, either cooked as a base to many dishes, or raw in salads.

Peanuts *Shing*: Classified as legumes, peanuts are native to south America and were spread worldwide by European traders. They are used in vegetable stuffings and as thickening agents in chutneys.

6 **Peas, Dried** *Vatana*: Dried peas, may be green or white.

Peppercorns *Kali Mirch*: This spice is used whole, ground or crushed in salads and main dishes. It is also used in spice blends such as garam masala, tea masala, chaat masala etc.

Pistachio *Pista*: This nut is originally from the area that is now Iran and Iraq. It is used in sweet dishes in Indian cuisine.

Poppy Seeds *Khus Khus*: The white variety of these small, round seeds is used in its whole form as a garnish on sweet dishes.

Potatoes *Aloo/Batata*: One of the most widely used and versatile ingredients in Indian cooking. It can be a main ingredient or added to vegetable dishes. Many of the recipes in this book contain potatoes. I highly recommend russet potatoes because they are creamy and not sticky.

21 **Red Chili Powder** *Mirchi*: Ground red chilies are used in many Indian dishes. They come in a variety of heat levels and the amount used can easily be varied based on the preferences and tolerances of each individual.

Rice, Basmati: This variety of rice has long grains and is the main variety of rice eaten in India. It has a distinct fragrance and flavor that goes well with all Indian Cuisine. You can buy both brown and white varieties, although the white is most common in India.

Rose Water *Gulabjal*: This liquid essence is used in desserts and lassis.

23 **Saffron** *Kesar*: Derived from the stamens of the saffron crocus, this spice is used to color and flavor savory and sweet dishes. It has lovely, distinct flavor and aroma when added to desserts. Strands are normally ground into a powder, then infused in milk to bring out the full flavor and color.

Sesame Seeds *Til*: Sesame seeds are quite tasteless in their raw state but have a wonderful nutty flavor when roasted and used in chakri. In addition, sesame oil is widely used in Indian cooking.

Seviyan **Vermicelli Noodles**: Thin, dried noodles, made from wheat flour.

Spinach *Saag*: This leafy green vegetable is used frequently in Indian cuisine and can be a substitute for fresh fenugreek (methi bhaji).

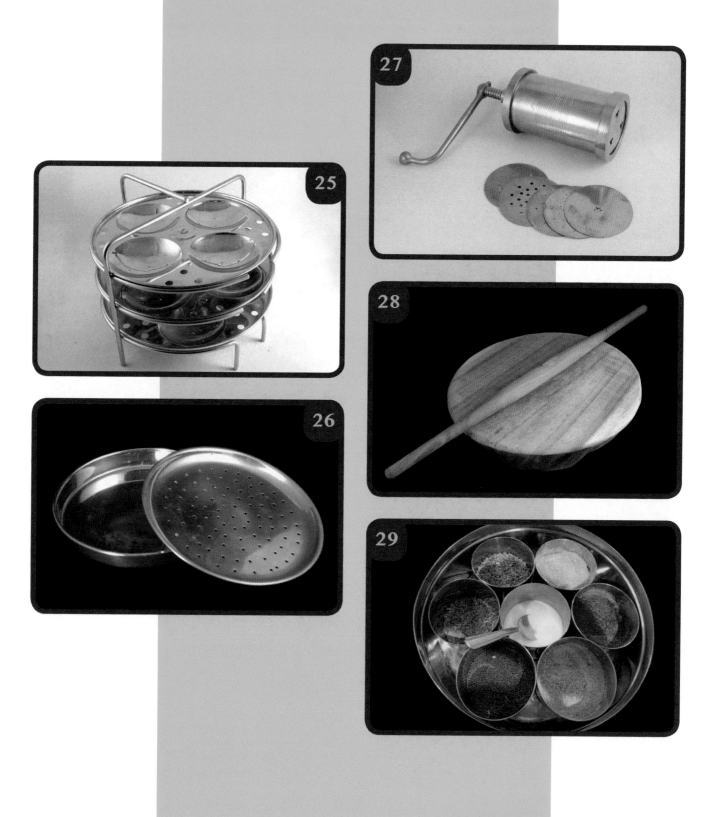

Tamarind *Imli*: This fruit is most often used as a souring agent. It can be used in its unripened, sour form in savory dishes, or when completely ripe and sweet as an ingredient in South Indian cuisine and chutneys.

(22) Tapioca *Sabudana*: Tapioca comes from the Manioc root. It can come in many forms and is often used as a thickening agent. In Indian cuisine, is is usually pearled. The small beads are typically soaked in water and then cooked.

(11) *Toor Daal* **Red Gram Daal/Split Pigeon Peas:** Skinned and split, toor daal is yellow and used in daals and South Indian sambar.

(24) Turmeric *Haldi*: A bright yellow root, turmeric is most often sold as a powdered spice. It is used mainly for color, rather than flavor, and has antiseptic properties. This spice stains hands and plastic containers easily.

(14) *Urad Daal* **White Lentils:** Typical of South Indian Cuisine. A small black legume which is creamy white when skinned and split. Used in idli, wada, dosa, etc.

Vinegar *Sirka*: White vinegar is used as a curdling agent when making paneer.

Specialty Tools

Any of these tools can be found at any Indian grocery or specialty store and can also be ordered online.

(25) (26) Idli/Dhokla/Moothia Steamer: This set of trays is used for steaming dishes such as Idli Khaman Dhokla, and Moothia. You can buy sets that include the different types of trays for each of the differnt dishes. It is typically set inside a large pot where a small quantity of water has been placed below.

(27) Chakri Maker *Chakri no Sancho*: This tool can be used to make a variety of fried snacks. It is used to make the appetizer Chakri. Alternatively, you can use a pastry bag fitted with an open star tip.

(28) Rolling Pin and Board *Belan & Patlo*: An Indian rolling pin and board are very useful tools for rolling any of the breads. Because of the rolling pin's unique tapered design, once you learn the technique, you can spin the bread as you roll, making perfect circles. The board helps with this special rolling technique, which is easier if your rolling surface is raised above the table.

(29) Spice Container *Masala Dhubha*: A round container with a lid, typically made of stainless steel, that holds seven open bowls with the most common spices used in Indian cooking — turmeric, red chili powder, coriander/cumin powder, salt, cumin seeds, mustard seeds, and fenugreek seeds.

BASIC METHODS & BLENDED SPICES

Basic Methods

Blended Spices

Temperature Chart for Deep Frying

450-500° high
375-400° medium-high
325-350° medium
275-300° medium-low
225-250° low

Choose an oil with a high smoke point, such as peanut oil, safflower oil, or canola oil.

High and medium-high heat is used when the frying time is very short, and a crispy and crunchy outer layer is desired.

Medium heat is used for foods with denser consistencies, that need a little longer frying time.

Medium-low and low heat is used to achieve a flaky outer crust and to keep the outside of the food from burning while the inside is still cooking.

Cooking Daals (Lentils and Legumes)

1 cup .... chickpeas, whole urad, dried peas (vatana)

1 For best results, rinse and soak overnight in 3 cups of water.
- If using a pressure cooker, stove top or electric, use the settings for legumes.
- If cooking on the stove top in a regular pot, add 1 more cup of water, cover and cook on low-medium heat for at least 1 hour or until tender.

1 cup .... chana daal, toor daal, moong daal, moong beans, lentils/masoor

1 For best results, rinse and add 3 cups of water.
- If using a pressure cooker, stove top or electric, use the settings for legumes.
- If cooking on the stove top in a regular pot, add 1 more cup of water, cover and cook on low-medium heat for at least 1 hour or until tender and mushy.

Boiling Potatoes

1 lb... potatoes (Will yield about two cups)

1. Russet potatoes are recommended for best results.

2. Boil potatoes in 4 cups of water for about 20-30 minutes or until cooked through. Pierce with a knife or fork to check if they are done.

3. Drain, then run under cold running water to stop the cooking process. Then peel off the skin, which should come off easily.

Caramelizing Onions

Caramelizing onions before adding to a recipe gives gravies a rich brown color.

If caramelizing on the stove:
- Add 2 tablespoons of oil in a heavy pan on medium to high heat. Fry onions until they are a rich, dark brown color. This may take 15 to 20 minutes.

If caramelizing in oven:
- Preheat oven to 450° F. Coat the onions in 2 tablespoons of oil and spread in a flat ovenproof tray. Bake for 15-20 minutes, checking every 5-10 minutes, until onions are nice and brown.

Making Ghee

1 lb... unsalted butter

1. Heat butter in a heavy pan on medium heat.

2. Once butter starts bubbling turn heat to low and let it simmer for 6-8 minutes or until clear.

3. When solids in butter start to turn light brown, ghee is ready.

4. Remove from heat immediately.

5. Strain with a fine mesh strainer and store in a glass jar. Refrigeration is not required.

BASIC METHODS
& INGREDIENTS

Making Paneer

4 cups .... whole milk (do not use ultra-pasteurized, it will not curdle)
3 T.. yogurt
1 T..lemon or lime juice

1 Grease heavy pan with a little butter or ghee to prevent the milk from sticking. Add milk and bring it to a boil over medium to high heat. Stir frequently while the milk is heating to prevent sticking and over-boiling.

2 Mix 3 tablespoons of yogurt in a small bowl until smooth. As soon as the milk starts to boil, add the yogurt while slowly stirring the milk. It should start to curdle. Add 1 tablespoon of lemon or lime juice. Once the curds separate and the whey is clear, turn off the heat.

3 Add 10-15 ice cubes, when ice cubes have melted, transfer curdled milk to cheesecloth to drain excess whey. Squeeze out the excess liquid by applying pressure to cheesecloth. Fold cheesecloth and form 4" X 4"x ½" thick block. Wrap a second, dry cheesecloth around it and press it to remove as much whey as possible. Set aside for 10-15 minutes before using.

Frying Paneer

1 Once the paneer has cooled completely, it can be pan fried.

2 Add 2 tablespoons of oil in a heavy pan and heat oil on medium heat.

3 When oil is heated, add paneer and sprinkle with 1/4 teaspoon salt. Fry 2-3 minutes on each side, until it browns.

Making Yogurt

4 cups .... 2% or higher fat milk (do not use ultra-pasteurized, it will not culture properly)
¼ cup .... plain yogurt

1 Grease heavy pan with a little butter or ghee, add 4 cups of milk and bring it to rolling boil on medium to high heat, stirring occasionally to prevent sticking. Transfer it to a glass bowl and set it aside until it is lukewarm.

2 Using a whisk or hand mixer, whisk the ¼ cup of yogurt until it is smooth.

3 Add the yogurt to the milk and incorporate with the whisk or hand mixer.

4 Place bowl in oven and heat oven on 350° for two minutes. Check after 6-8 hours. If milk is still runny, heat oven for two minutes again. Check after 6-8 hours, yogurt should be ready. Refrigerate and use within 5-7 days.

BASIC METHODS
& INGREDIENTS

Preparing Saffron

1. Heat a small heavy pan on medium heat, then add saffron strands.
2. When saffron start to darken, remove from heat, and add 2 tablespoons of milk.
3. Mix until the milk turns yellow, then set aside.

Roasting Cumin

1. Heat a small heavy pan on medium heat, add ½ cup cumin seeds.
2. Roast for 3-4 minutes or until cumin starts to turn brown and become fragrant.

Sprouting Moong Beans

1/2 cup .... moong beans

1. Wash moong beans and soak in two cups of lukewarm water for at least 3-4 hours.
2. Drain and place the moong beans in a metal colander. Place colander in the oven and heat on 350° for two minutes. Leave moong beans in the oven for 12 hours.
3. Sprinkle 3-4 tablespoons of water over the beans and leave them in the oven for another 12 hours. Once they sprout, they will be ready to eat. You can eat them raw in salads.

BASIC METHODS
& INGREDIENTS

All of the blended spices in this section can be purchased pre-packaged at any Indian grocery store. The lists below provide the ingredients in each blended spice mixture for your information. You can also make your own if you choose to do so. Homemade blends should be used within 6 months for optimal freshness and flavor.

Garam Masala

5-6	sticks cinnamon
1 T	cardamom seeds
20-25	cloves
2 T	whole black peppercorns
2 T	cumin seeds
1 t	nutmeg powder

Roast all ingredients together in a skillet for 2 minutes on low heat, stirring constantly until fragrant. Remove from heat, cool, and grind to a fine powder in a spice grinder. Store in a glass jar.

Chaat Masala

3 T	cumin seeds
2 t	carom seeds
1 T	ginger powder
2 t	mango powder
2 t	black salt
1 t	ground black pepper
½ t	nutmeg powder

Roast cumin and carom seeds in a small skillet until brown.
Grind roasted seeds and mix in the remaining ingredients. Store in a glass jar.

Chai Masala

4 T	ginger powder
1 T	cardamom powder
1 T	cinnamon powder
1 t	clove powder
1 t	nutmeg powder

Combine all ingredients and store in a glass jar. See chai recipe on page 23.

Sambhar Powder

1 t	oil
1 T	chana daal
1/4 cup	coriander seeds
1 T	cumin seeds
2 T	fenugreek seeds
5-6	dry red chilies
½ t	asafetida
1 T	whole black peppercorns

In a nonstick skillet, heat the oil and add the chana daal. Cook for 2-3 minutes until the daal turns brown. Add the rest of the ingredients and roast for an additional 2-3 minutes. Cool , then grind to a fine powder. Store in a glass jar.

Tandoori Masala

2 T	coriander seeds
2 T	cumin seeds
1 T	fenugreek seeds
1 T	whole black peppercorns
1 T	cloves
1 T	cardamom seeds
2 T	red chili powder
1 T	cinnamon powder
1 T	ginger powder

In a nonstick skillet, roast together all the ingredients until fragrant. Remove from heat and let the spices cool down, Grind to a fine powder. Store in a glass jar.

BASIC METHODS
& INGREDIENTS

Chai

Ingredients

2 cups ....water

2 cups .... low fat milk (1% or 2%)

OR

3 cups ....water

1 cup.. full fat milk

¼ t... chai masala

1 t .... grated ginger (optional)

1 t .... finely chopped mint (optional)

½ t........... finely chopped lemon grass (optional)

4 t .... loose black tea leaves or 5 black tea bags

4 t ....sugar (or sweeter to taste)

Method

1 Bring water to boil in a pot. Add chai masala, ginger, mint and lemon grass. Simmer for 1-2 minutes. Add black tea and simmer for an additional 1-2 minutes. Add milk and sugar and bring it to boil. Watch the pot, as it will boil over easily and without much warning. Once it has boiled, remove from heat, cover, and set aside for 2-3 minutes.

2 Strain with a fine strainer to remove all the solid spices.

3 Chai goes well with salty snacks or sweet biscuits. It is great on a cold day to warm you up and makes a perfect after-dinner drink, with or without dessert.

DAHI WADA - PAGE 30

POTATO WADA - PAGE 37

VEGETABLE & FRUIT CHAT -
PAGE 41

SABUDANA WADA - PAGE 38

CHAPTER 1: APPETIZERS

The recipes in this section are normally finger foods that make ideal starters to any meal. When the weather is cold and rainy, fried pakodas are the perfect food to warm you up. Always keep cilantro chutney or tamarind chutney on hand in your freezer. In the absence of chutney, sprinkle some chaat masala on top. Pakodas are considered street food in India and if you are travelling there, freshly fried, they are usually the safest foods to eat because of the high heat of deep frying (minus the chutney, of course). These appetizers are my family's comfort foods. Occasionally we even make an entire meal out of them.

CHAKRI - PAGE 27

CORN PAKODA - PAGE 29

MASALA WADA - PAGE 33

ONION PAKODA - PAGE 35

Chakri

Serves 12
Preparation time: 15 minutes
Cooking time: 20 minutes

Vegetarian

Gluten free

Calories 270 • Calories from Fat 160 • Total Fat 18g (Saturated Fat 3.5g, Trans Fat 0g) • Cholesterol 5mg • Sodium 420mg • Total Carbohydrates 23g (Dietary Fiber 1g, Sugars 2g) • Protein 3g

Ingredients

2 cups .... rice flour	¼ cup .... crushed sesame seeds
2 T... urad flour	1 t .... red chili powder
2 T... butter	1 T.............. crushed ajwain seeds (carom seeds)
2 t .... salt	1½ cups.. buttermilk

Approx 2 cups of oil for deep frying

Method

1. Combine all the ingredients in a bowl to make the chakri dough. It should be the consistency of play dough.

2. Cover the bowl with wet cloth and set aside for at least one hour.

3. Fill dough in chakri maker (page 13) or a pastry bag fitted with an open star tip, create swirls 2-3" in diameter (see picture on opposite page) on a cookie sheet or cutting board.

4. Heat oil in frying pan on medium (325°) heat.

5. Using a spatula, carefully pick up each swirl and place in the oil. Fry 6-8 pieces of chakris at a time for 3-4 minutes or until the color changes to a light golden brown. Move the chakris around and flip occasionally to ensure even cooking. Continue making and frying the chakris until the dough is all gone.

6. Let them cool before storing the chakris in an air tight container. They will stay good for 2-3 weeks.

Chicken & Paneer Pakoda

Gluten free

Serves 8
Preparation time: 45 minutes
Cooking time: 30 minutes

Calories 260 • Calories from Fat 100 • Total Fat 11g (Saturated Fat 5g, Trans Fat 0g) • Cholesterol 55mg Sodium 340mg • Total Carbohydrates 22g (Dietary Fiber 3g, Sugars 3g) • Protein 17g

Ingredients

Marinade

¼ cup each	ginger, garlic, & jalapeno
1 t	garam masala
1 T	lemon juice
½ t	salt
¼ cup	water

• • •

1 cup	fried paneer, cut into 1" x ½" pieces (page 19)
½ lb	boneless, skinless chicken cut into 1" pieces

• • •

Batter

2 cups	besan
½ cup	rice flour
1 t	red chili powder
½ t	turmeric
1 T	coriander powder
1 t	salt
⅛ t	baking soda
1 ½ cups	water (as needed)

• • •

1 t	chaat masala

• • •

Approx 2 cups of oil for deep frying

Method

1. Combine all the ingredients for marinade in a mini food processor and process for 1-2 minutes. Divide the marinade in two parts and transfer to separate bowls. Add chicken to one part and paneer to the other part. Cover and set aside for at least 30 minutes.

2. In a separate bowl, combine all the batter ingredients with a wisk. It will form a smooth batter that is thick enough to coat the back of a spoon. Set aside for 20-30 minutes.

3. Heat oil in frying pan on medium high (375°) heat.

4. Dip the marinated chicken and paneer pieces in the batter and fry 8-10 pakodas for 3-4 minutes or until brown and crispy. Drain on paper towels. Continue frying rest of the pakodas.

5. Sprinkle chaat masala on top and serve with cilantro chutney (page 60).

Corn Pakoda

Serves 8
Preparation time: 15 minutes
Cooking time: 20 minutes

Vegan

Vegetarian

Calories 240 • Calories from Fat 130 • Total Fat 15g (Saturated Fat 2g, Trans Fat 0g) • Cholesterol 0mg • Sodium 480mg • Total Carbohydrates 24g (Dietary Fiber 2g, Sugars 1g) • Protein 4g • Provides 35% of daily iron needs

Ingredients

1 cup .... corn kernels

1 cup .... cream of wheat

½ cup .... besan

½ cup .... water (as needed)

¼ cup .... finely chopped jalapeno

2 T.................................... finely chopped ginger

1 t .... garam masala

¼ cup .... finely chopped cilantro

1 ½ t.. salt

¼ t... baking soda

• • •

1 t .... chaat masala

• • •

Approx 2 cups of oil for deep frying

Method

1 Crush corn in a mini food processor.

2 Transfer to a mixing bowl, add rest of the ingredients. Dough should be soft but should still hold its shape when you form small balls.

3 Heat oil in frying pan on medium high (375°) heat.

4 Apply water to your fingers, take a tablespoon of the mixture and form a round ball. Fry 10-12 pakodas for 3-4 minutes or until golden brown and crunchy. Drain on paper towels. Continue frying the pakodas until the dough is all gone.

5 Sprinkle chaat masala on top and serve with cilantro chutney (page 60).

Dahi Wada

Vegetarian

Gluten free

Serves 8
Preparation time: 30 minutes
Cooking time: 30 minutes

Calories 330 • Calories from Fat 160 • Total Fat 18g (Saturated Fat 3.5g, Trans Fat 0g) • Cholesterol 10mg Sodium 300mg • Total Carbohydrates 27g (Dietary Fiber 8g, Sugars 8g) • Protein 12g • 20% calcium needs

Ingredients

1 cup	moong daal
½ cup	urad daal
2 t	salt
¼ cup	chopped cashews
½ cup	finely chopped jalapeno

• • •

¼ t	salt
3 cups	yogurt

Garnish

½ cup	date or tamarind chutney (page 61)
½ cup	cilantro chutney (page 60)
1 t	roasted ground cumin powder (page 20)
½ t	red chili powder
2 T	finely chopped cilantro

• • •

Approx 2 cups of oil for deep frying

Method

1. Rinse and soak moong daal and urad daal in lukewarm water for at least 3-4 hours.

2. Drain and puree soaked daal in a blender or food processor. Add ¼ cup water or as needed so you can easily slide the mixture into the oil with a spoon.

3. Transfer the mixture to a bowl and add 2 teaspoons of salt, cashews, and jalapeno and mix well. Fill a four quart bowl with cold water and set near the stove.

4. Heat oil in frying pan on medium high (375°) heat.

5. Dip a dinner spoon in water then take a spoonful of batter and place into the hot oil. The mixture will slide off the spoon. Fry 10-12 wadas for 3-4 minutes or until golden brown and crunchy. Immediately put the wadas in a bowl of cold water to soak. Continue frying the wadas until the batter is all gone.

6. Soak wada for at least 15-20 minutes, until soft. Gently squeeze each wada to remove extra water. Arrange wadas in a shallow glass plate.

7. In a bowl mix yogurt and ¼ teaspoon salt. Pour the yogurt mixture on top of wada. Garnish with date or tamarind chutney, cilantro chutney, roasted cumin powder, red chili powder, and cilantro.

8. Refrigerate to serve later or serve immediately.

30

CHAPTER 1
APPETIZERS

Khaman Dhokla

Serves 8
Preparation time: 15 minutes
Cooking time: 25 minutes

Vegan

Vegetarian

Gluten free

Ingredients

1 ½ cups...besan	¼ cup ....oil
1 cup...water	1 t ....mustard seeds
1 t ....salt	10-12 pieces ....limdo/curry leaves
2 t ....sugar	1/8 t ....asafetida
½ t...baking soda	1 cup...water
2 T...lemon or lime juice	1 t ....sugar
• • •	1 T..lime or lemon juice
	¼ cup ....finely chopped jalapeno
	¼ cup ....finely chopped cilantro

Method

1. Boil water on medium heat in a large pot big enough to fit an 8-9" round pie plate or cake pan for steaming.

2. Combine besan, water, and salt in a large bowl. Add sugar, baking soda, and lemon or lime juice on top of mixture. Mix vigorously with a whisk until the batter is frothy and smooth.

3. Oil the round plate with ½ teaspoon of oil. Pour mixture in the pan and place in steamer and steam for 15 minutes until cooked.

4. Prepare seasoning while khaman is cooking.
   In a small pan heat ¼ cup of oil. Add mustard seeds. When mustard seeds start crackling, add limdo/curry leaves, asafetida, and 1 cup water. Bring it to boil then add sugar, lemon or lime juice, finely chopped jalapeno and cilantro. Set aside.

5. Check khaman by inserting a knife in the middle, if the knife comes out, clean the khaman is ready. If not continue to steam for an additional 2-3 minutes.

6. Remove the plate from the pot and allow it to cool for 5 minutes.

7. Turn the plate upside down over a cutting board. The khaman will come out. It will be nice and spongy. Cut into 1-2" pieces with a sharp knife and transfer to a mixing bowl. Gradually pour the seasoning mixture on top of khaman and gently toss it.

8. Serve with cilantro chutney (page 60).

Kheema Samosa

Serves 12
Preparation time: 30 minutes
Cooking time: 30 minutes

Calories 320 • Calories from Fat 190 • Total Fat 22g (Saturated Fat 3.5g, Trans Fat 0g) • Cholesterol 25mg • Sodium 430mg • Total Carbohydrates 22g (Dietary Fiber 2g, Sugars 1g) • Protein 12g

Ingredients

Approx 2 cups of oil for deep frying

• • •

Dough

1 cup each	all purpose flour & whole wheat flour
1 t	salt
¼ t	baking soda
4 T	oil
1 cup	water (as needed)

• • •

Stuffing

1 lb	ground lamb/turkey/beef
1 cup	finely chopped onion
¼ cup each	finely chopped garlic & jalapeno
1 t	garam masala
½ t	red chili powder
1 t	salt
1 cup	green peas
1 T	lime or lemon juice
¼ cup	water

Method

1. Combine all the dough ingredients in a mixing bowl. It should be the consistency of play dough. Cover and set aside for 30 minutes.

2. In a heavy skillet over medium heat, cook ground meat until mostly cooked through, breaking the meat apart with a wooden spoon until crumbled. Transfer cooked meat to a bowl, and drain off all but approximately 1 tablespoon of fat.

3. Cook onion in that fat for 4-5 minutes. Add garlic and cook for 1-2 minutes. Add jalapeno, garam masala, red chili powder, salt and peas, and cook for 2-3 minutes. Return the browned meat to the skillet, and add lime and or lemon juice and ¼ cup of water. Reduce heat to low and simmer, uncovered, for 5 to 10 minutes or until meat is fully cooked, stirring occasionally to prevent sticking. The mixture should be dry. Let the meat cool for at least 15 minutes before stuffing.

4. Knead dough for 3-4 minutes until the dough becomes smooth and elastic. Divide dough into 12 equal portions. Divide stuffing into 24 equal portions. Roll dough into about 4" to 5" rounds. Cut in half. Shape each semicircle into cones by folding the flat edges over each other, leaving an opening at the top. Pinch and seal the sides. Stuff with mixture. Apply a little water to the top edges and seal the samosa. Arrange samosas on wax paper.

5. Heat oil in frying pan on medium low (325°) heat.

6. Pinch sides again as you fry 5-6 samosas for about 3-4 minute on each side. The crust will be golden and flaky.

7. Serve with cilantro chutney (page 60).

Masala Wada

Vegan

Vegetarian

Gluten free

Serves 8
Preparation time: 15 minutes
Cooking time: 20 minutes

Calories 260 • Calories from Fat 140 • Total Fat 15g (Saturated Fat 2g, Trans Fat 0g) • Cholesterol 0mg • Sodium 443mg • Total Carbohydrates 24g (Dietary Fiber 8g, Sugars 4g) • Protein 10g

Ingredients

½ cup each............................uncooked toor daal, urad daal, & chana daal

1 tsp......................... crushed red pepper

½ cup each................................... finely chopped jalapeno & onion

8-10 pieces .... limdo/curry leaves

¼ cup .... finely chopped ginger

1 ½ t.. salt

• • •

1 t ....chaat masala

• • •

Approx 2 cups of oil for deep frying

Method

Note: Soak toor daal, urad daal, and chana daal for at least 2-3 hours in lukewarm water.

1. Drain all the water and grind to a coarse mixture in a food processor. Transfer the mixture to a bowl, add the rest of the ingredients, and mix well.

2. Heat oil in frying pan on medium high (375°) heat.

3. Apply water to your fingers, take a tablespoon of the mixture, form a round ball, and then pat it down to flatten it. Gently place in the oil. Fry 6-8 wadas for 3-4 minutes or until golden brown and crunchy.

4. Sprinkle chaat masala on top and enjoy with coconut chutney (page 60).

Moothia

Vegetarian

Serves 8
Preparation time: 15 minutes
Cooking time: 20 minutes

Calories 160 • Calories from Fat 60 • Total Fat 6g (Saturated Fat 0.5g, Trans Fat 0g) • Cholesterol 0mg • Sodium 360mg • Total Carbohydrates 21g (Dietary Fiber 2g, Sugars 2g) • Protein 5g

Ingredients

1 cup	chopped spinach/methi bhaji, cabbage, zucchini, or doodhi
1 cup	cream of wheat
½ cup	besan
¼ cup	finely chopped jalapeno
½ cup	yogurt
1 ½ t	salt
½ t	turmeric
2 T	oil
¼ t	baking soda
½ cup	water (as needed)

• • •

Garnish

1 T	oil
1 t	mustard seeds
¼ cup	finely chopped cilantro

Method

1. Combine all the ingredients in a mixing bowl. Dough should hold its shape when you form long rolls, but still be slightly sticky.

2. Use a vegetable steamer to steam the moothia. Divide mixture in 4-5 portions. Make about 6" long rolls in palm of your hand and arrange them side by side in the steamer basket. Steam for about 20 minutes.

3. Remove from heat and set aside to cool for 15-20 minutes. Cut into 1" pieces with knife.

4. Heat 1 tablespoon of oil in a nonstick pan on medium high heat. Add 1 teaspoon mustard seeds. When they begin to crackle, add the sliced moothia to the pan and gently toss it. Garnish with cilantro.

5. Serve with cilantro chutney (page 60).

Onion Pakoda

Serves 8
Preparation time: 15 minutes
Cooking time: 20 minutes

Vegan

Vegetarian

Gluten Free

Calories 240 • Calories from Fat 140 • Total Fat 16g (Saturated Fat 2g, Trans Fat 0g) • Cholesterol 0mg • Sodium 450mg • Total Carbohydrates 17g (Dietary Fiber 3g, Sugars 4g) • Protein 6g • 30% Vitamin C

Ingredients

2 cups .... besan

2 cups .... thin long slices of vidalia or sweet white onion

1 cup................................. thinly sliced jalapeno (if you want it nice and hot) OR thinly sliced bell pepper OR combination of both

½ cup .... finely chopped cilantro

2 T.. lime or lemon juice

1 ½ t.. salt

• • •

1 t .... chaat masala

• • •

Approx 2 cups of oil for deep frying

Method

1. Mix all the ingredients in a mixing bowl with a wooden spoon. If the mixture is stiff and crumbly, add 1 to 2 tablespoons of water at a time until it comes together.

2. Heat oil in frying pan on medium high (375°) heat.

3. Apply some oil on your fingers, take a spoonful of mixture, place on your fingers and pat it down. Fry 6-8 pakodas for 3-4 minutes until golden brown. Drain on paper towel. Repeat with all the dough.

4. Sprinkle chaat masala on top and serve with cilantro chutney (page 60).

VEGETABLE POODLA - PAGE 44

VEGETABLE SAMOSA - PAGE 45

VEGETABLE CUTLETS - PAGE 42

VEGETABLE SAMOSA STUFFING

Potato Wada

Serves 8
Preparation time: 45 minutes
Cooking time: 20 minutes

Vegan

Vegetarian

Gluten free

Calories 280 • Calories from Fat 170 • Total Fat 19g (Saturated Fat 2.5g, Trans Fat 0g) • Cholesterol 0mg • Sodium 610mg • Total Carbohydrates 20g (Dietary Fiber 3g, Sugars 3g) • Protein 6g

Ingredients

1 lb	russet potatoes

• • •

Batter

2 cups	besan
¼ t	baking soda
½ t	red chili powder
½ t	garam masala
½ t	turmeric
1 T	coriander powder
2 T	lemon or lime juice
1 t	salt
1 ½ cups	water (as needed)

• • •

2 T	oil
2 T	urad daal
1 t	mustard seeds
¼ t	asafetida
8 to 10 leaves	limdo/curry leaves
2 T	finely chopped ginger
¼ cup each	finely chopped jalapeno & cilantro
2 T	lime or lemon juice
1 t	salt

• • •

Approx 2 cups of oil for deep frying

Method

1. Boil 1 lb of russet potatoes in 4 cups of water for about 20-30 minutes or until cooked. After they finish cooking, run them under cold running water to stop the cooking process. Then peel and coarsely mash with a potato masher. This will yield about two cups of coarsely mashed potatoes.

2. In a separate bowl, combine all the ingredients for the batter with a whisk. It will form a smooth batter that is thick enough to coat the back of a spoon. Set aside for 20-30 minutes.

3. Heat 2 tablespoons of oil in a pan on medium high heat. Add urad daal and mustard seeds. When urad daal turns light brown and mustard seeds start crackling, add asafetida, limdo/curry leaves, ginger, jalapeno, cilantro, lime or lemon juice, mashed potatoes, and salt. Remove from heat and mix well.

4. Divide potato mixture in 24 equal parts. Apply some oil to your palm and take one part of mixture and form smooth round balls. Arrange on a cookie sheet.

5. Heat the oil in frying pan on medium high (375°) heat.

6. Place each ball in the batter and cover it completely, then put it in the hot oil. Fry 8-10 wadas at a time for 3-4 minutes or until golden brown.

7. Serve with cilantro chutney (page 60).

Sabudana Wada

Vegan

Vegetarian

Gluten free

Serves 8
Preparation time: 45 minutes
Cooking time: 20 minutes

Calories 230 • Calories from Fat 170 • Total Fat 19g (Saturated Fat 2.5g, Trans Fat 0g) • Cholesterol 0mg • Sodium 440mg • Total Carbohydrates 19g (Dietary Fiber 2g, Sugars 1g) • Protein 3g

Ingredients

½ cup .... sabudana/tapioca

1 cup...water

• • •

1 lb.. russet potatoes

½ cup .... coarsely grounded roasted peanuts

½ cup .... finely chopped cilantro

¼ cup .... finely chopped jalapeno

1 t ....garam masala

¼ cup .... corn starch

2 T... lime or lemon juice

1 ½ t... salt

• • •

Approx 2 cups of oil for deep frying

Method

Note: Soak sabudana/tapioca for at least 1 hour in 1 cup of lukewarm water in a mixing bowl.

1. Boil 1 lb of russet potatoes in 4 cups of water for about 20-30 minutes or until cooked. After they finish cooking, run them under cold running water to stop the cooking process. Then peel and coarsely mash with a potato masher. This will yield about two cups of coarsely mashed potatoes.

2. Drain excess water from sabudana/tapioca and add mashed potato and rest of the ingredients. The mixture will be lumpy.

3. Heat oil in frying pan on medium high (375°) heat.

4. Apply a little oil on your palm and make 1" round and ½" thick flat wada. Arrange wadas on a cookie sheet. Fry 6-8 wadas at a time for 3-4 minutes until golden brown.

5. Serve with cilantro chutney (page 60).

Sakkarpara: Sweet or Salty

Serves 12
Preparation time: 20 minutes
Cooking time: 30 minutes

Vegetarian

SWEET: Calories 230 • Calories from Fat 100 • Total Fat 11g (Saturated Fat 3.5g, Trans Fat 0g) • Cholesterol 10mg • Sodium 10mg • Total Carbohydrates 31g (Dietary Fiber 1g, Sugars 18g) • Protein 2g

SALTY: Calories 170 • Calories from Fat 100 • Total Fat 11g (Saturated Fat 3.5g, Trans Fat 0g) • Cholesterol 10mg • Sodium 300mg • Total Carbohydrates 14g (Dietary Fiber 1g, Sugars 1g) • Protein 2g

Ingredients

Approx 2 cups of oil for deep frying

• • •

Sweet
½ cup ....cream of wheat
1 cup.. sugar
¾ cup .... milk (as needed)
1 cup...............................all purpose flour
¼ cup .... butter

Salty
½ cup ....cream of wheat
¾ cup .... milk (as needed)
1 cup..all purpose flour
1 ½ t... salt
¼ cup .... butter
1 t .... black pepper
1 t .... red chili powder
1 t ....cumin powder

Method

1. For sweet Sakkarpara:
Combine cream of wheat, sugar, and milk. Mix well and set aside for 5 minutes. Add all purpose flour and butter to prepare dough that is the consistency of pie crust. Cover and set aside for at least ½ hour.

2. For salty Sakkarpara:
Combine cream of wheat and milk, mix well, and set aside for 5 minutes. Add rest of the ingredients to prepare dough that is the consistency of pie crust. Cover and set aside for at least ½ hour.

3. Knead dough for 3-4 minutes then divide into 6-8 equal parts. Roll into about 6-8" rounds. Cut into 1" squares using pizza cutter.

4. Heat oil in frying pan on medium (350°) heat. Add the squares to frying pan and fry for 4-5 minutes or until golden brown. They will float to the top of the oil when done. Move around and flip occasionally to ensure even cooking. Repeat for rest of the dough.

5. Let cool before storing in air tight container. They will stay good for 2-3 weeks.

Spinach Pakoda

Vegan

Vegetarian

Serves 8
Preparation time: 20 minutes
Cooking time: 20 minutes

Calories 300 • Calories from Fat 180 • Total Fat 20g (Saturated Fat 3g, Trans Fat 0g) • Cholesterol 0mg • Sodium 660mg • Total Carbohydrates 20g (Dietary Fiber 2g, Sugars 1g) • Protein 4g • 35% iron

Ingredients

2 cups .... finely chopped spinach	1 t .... garam masala
1 cup .... cream of wheat	1 ½ t .... salt
½ cup .... besan	⅛ t .... baking soda
3 T .... oil	2 T .... lemon or lime juice
¼ cup .... finely chopped jalapeno	• • •

Approx 2 cups of oil for deep frying

Method

1. Combine all the ingredients in a mixing bowl. Add 1 to 2 tablespoons of water as needed to form a sticky dough. The mixture should hold its shape when you form it into balls.

2. Heat oil in frying pan on medium high (375°) heat.

3. Apply some oil on your fingers, take about 1 tablespoon of mixture, shape it into a ball with your fingers, and place it in the hot oil. Fry 8-10 pakodas for 3-4 minutes until golden brown and crunchy. Repeat for rest of the dough.

4. Serve with cilantro chutney (page 60).

Vegetable & Fruit Chaat

Serves 12
Preparation time: 20 minutes
Cooking time: 20 minutes

Vegan

Vegetarian

Gluten free

A perfect appetizer or side dish for a hot summer evening.

Calories 60 • Calories from Fat 25 • Total Fat 2.5g (Saturated Fat 0g, Trans Fat 0g) • Cholesterol 0mg • Sodium 0mg • Total Carbohydrates 9g (Dietary Fiber 1g, Sugars 4g) • Protein 1g

Ingredients

Seasoning

½ t.. red chili powder
½ t....................................roasted cumin powder
½ cup .... finely chopped cilantro
2 T...chaat masala
2 T................................... lime or lemon juice
2 T...olive oil
• • •

Cut into bite size cubes

1 cup each ....boiled potato, cucumber, cherry tomatoes, banana, apple, & grapes

OR

1 cup each ....kiwi, mango, pineapple, pear or other fruit of your choice
• • •

8-10 leaves ....finely chopped fresh mint

Method

1 Combine all the seasoning ingredients in a bowl with a whisk.

2 Combine all the fruits and vegetables in a serving bowl. Pour the seasoning mixture on top and toss well.

3 Decorate with chopped mint.

4 Serve immediately or can be refrigerated for up to an hour and served cold.

Vegetable Cutlets

Vegan

Vegetarian

Serves 12
Preparation time: 30 minutes
Cooking time: 30 minutes

Calories 240 • Calories from Fat 130 • Total Fat 15g (Saturated Fat 2g, Trans Fat 0g) • Cholesterol 0mg • Sodium 270mg • Total Carbohydrates 22g (Dietary Fiber 2g, Sugars 2g) • Protein 3g • 20% Vitamin C, 25% Vitamin A

Ingredients

1 lb... russet potatoes	1 t .... salt
2 cups ....mixed vegetables (peas, carrots, corn and green beans)	• • •
½ cup ....finely chopped cabbage	1 cup..bread crumbs
¼ cup each................................ finely chopped ginger, jalapeno, & cilantro	4-5 ....leaves of lettuce
	1 cup...tomato slices
1 t ....garam masala	½ cup .... onion slices
½ cup .... cornstarch	• • •
2 T...lime or lemon juice	Approx 2 cups of oil for deep frying - OR use griddle or skillet to pan fry

Method

1. Boil 1 lb of russet potatoes in 4 cups of water for about 20-30 minutes or until cooked. After they finish cooking, run them under cold running water to stop the cooking process. Then peel and mash with a potato masher. This will yield about two cups of mashed potatoes.

2. Boil mixed vegetables for 5-7 minutes, until soft. Transfer vegetables to colander and squeeze out extra water. Set aside until cool.

3. Combine mashed potatoes, boiled vegetables, chopped cabbage, ginger, jalapeno, cilantro, garam masala, corn starch, lemon or lime juice, and salt in a mixing bowl.

4. Divide mixture in 24 parts.

5. To cook patties on griddle or skillet:
   - Heat skillet or griddle on medium heat. Take one part mixture and shape into a circular flat patty. Roll it in bread crumbs and shake off the excess. Arrange cutlets in a cookie sheet.
   - With a pastry brush apply some oil on one side of patty. Place the oil side on the skillet or griddle. Place several patties at a time. Cook for 3-4 minutes, apply oil to the top, flip, and cook an additional 3-4 minutes until golden brown.

6. To deep fry patties:
   - Take one part of mixture and shape into a circular flat patty. Roll it in bread crumbs and shake off the excess. Arrange cutlets in a cookie sheet.
   - Heat oil in frying pan on medium high (375°) heat and fry 5-6 pieces of cutlets for 3-4 minutes until bread crumbs starts to turn brown, turning once halfway through. Drain on paper towels.

7. In a serving plate, place whole lettuce leaves, onion, and tomatoes slices. Arrange patties on top and serve with ketchup or cilantro chutney (page 60).

8. You can also use the cutlets as veggie burgers, with a grilled bun, lettuce, tomatoes, and onion.

Vegetable Pakoda

Serves 8
Preparation time: 30 minutes
Cook Time: 30 minutes

Vegan

Vegetarian

Gluten free

Calories 250 • Calories from Fat 140 • Total Fat 16g (Saturated Fat 2g, Trans Fat 0g) • Cholesterol 0mg • Sodium 310mg • Total Carbohydrates 21g (Dietary Fiber 4g, Sugars 4g) • Protein 6g • 30% Vitamin C

Ingredients

Batter

2 cups	besan
½ cup	rice flour
1 t	salt
½ t	garam masala
½ t	turmeric
½ t	red chili powder
1 T	lime or lemon juice
1 cup	water (as needed)

• • •

1 medium	thinly sliced potato
1 medium	thinly sliced onion
1	thinly sliced bell pepper
½ t	salt

• • •

1 t	chaat masala

• • •

Approx 2 cups of oil for deep frying

Method

1. In a bowl, combine all the ingredients for the batter with a whisk. It will form a smooth batter that is thick enough to coat the back of a spoon. Set aside for 20-30 minutes.

2. Thinly slice all the vegetables and sprinkle ½ teaspoon of salt. Cover and set aside.

3. Heat oil in frying pan on medium high (375°) heat.

4. Dip the vegetable slices in the batter and fry 8-10 pakodas for 3-4 minutes or until brown and crispy. Drain on paper towels. Continue frying the rest of the pakodas.

5. Sprinkle chaat masala on top and serve with cilantro chutney (page 60).

Vegetable Poodla

Vegan

Vegetarian

Gluten free

Can be used as a gluten free bread.

Serves 8
Preparation time: 15 minutes
Cooking time: 20 minutes

Calories 110 • Calories from Fat 15 • Total Fat 1.5g (Saturated Fat 0g, Trans Fat 0g) • Cholesterol 0mg • Sodium 610mg • Total Carbohydrates 17g (Dietary Fiber 8g, Sugars 4g) • Protein 6g

Ingredients

2 cups .... besan
½ cup each......................... finely chopped onion, tomato, green bell pepper, carrots, cauliflower, & cilantro
1 t .... red chili powder
1 t .... turmeric

1 t .... garam masala
2 T............................. lime or lemon juice
2 t .... salt
1 cup................................ water (as needed)

• • •

¼ cup .... oil for pan frying

Method

1. Combine all the ingredients in a mixing bowl. This will make a thick, pourable batter, the consistency of pancake batter. Set aside for 10-15 minutes.

2. Heat a griddle or skillet on medium high heat. Apply ½ teaspoon oil and cover the cooking surface. Pour ¾ cup of batter and spread with spatula. Cook 2-3 minutes on one side and apply oil with a pastry brush on the top side. Turn poodla over and cook for 2-3 minutes or until edges starts turning brown.

3. Serve with cilantro chutney (page 60).

Vegetable Samosa

Vegan

Vegetarian

Serves 12
Preparation time: 45 minutes
Cooking time: 30 minutes

Calories 340 • Calories from Fat 210 • Total Fat 23g (Saturated Fat 3.5g, Trans Fat 0g) • Cholesterol 0mg • Sodium 500mg • Total Carbohydrates 28g (Dietary Fiber 3g, Sugars 1g) • Protein 4g

Ingredients

Dough

1 cup each	all purpose flour & whole wheat flour
1 t	salt
¼ t	baking soda
4 T	oil
½ cup	water (as needed)

• • •

Stuffing

1 lb	russet potatoes
2 T	oil
½ t	cumin seeds
¼ cup	cashew pieces
1 cup	green peas
¼ cup each	finely chopped ginger & jalapeno
1 t	garam masala
½ t	red chili powder
¼ cup	cilantro
1 ½ t	salt
2 T	lime or lemon juice

• • •

Approx 2 cups of oil for deep frying

Method

1. In a bowl combine all the dough ingredients. It should be the consistency of play dough. Cover and set aside for 30 minutes.

2. Boil 1 lb of russet potatoes in 4 cups of water for about 20-30 minutes or until cooked. After they finish cooking, run them under cold running water to stop the cooking process. Then peel and coarsely mash with a potato masher. This will yield about two cups of coarsely mashed potatoes.

3. Heat 2 tablespoons of oil in a pan on medium high heat. Add cumin seeds and when brown, add cashews and cook for one more minute. Add green peas, ginger, jalapeno, garam masala, red chili powder, mashed potatoes, cilantro, salt, and lime or lemon juice. Turn off the stove. Mix all the ingredients and let it cool for 15 minutes. It will be ready for stuffing samosas.

4. Knead dough for 3-4 minutes until the dough becomes smooth and elastic. Divide dough into 12 equal portions. Divide stuffing into 24 equal portions. Roll dough into about 4" to 5" rounds. Cut in half. Shape each semicircle into cones by folding the flat edges over each other, leaving an opening at the top. Pinch and seal the sides. Stuff with mixture. Apply a little water to the top edges and seal the samosa. Arrange samosas on wax paper.

5. Heat oil in frying pan on medium low (325°) heat.

6. Pinch sides again as you fry 5-6 samosas for 3-4 minute on each side. The crust will be golden and flaky.

6. Serve with cilantro chutney (page 60).

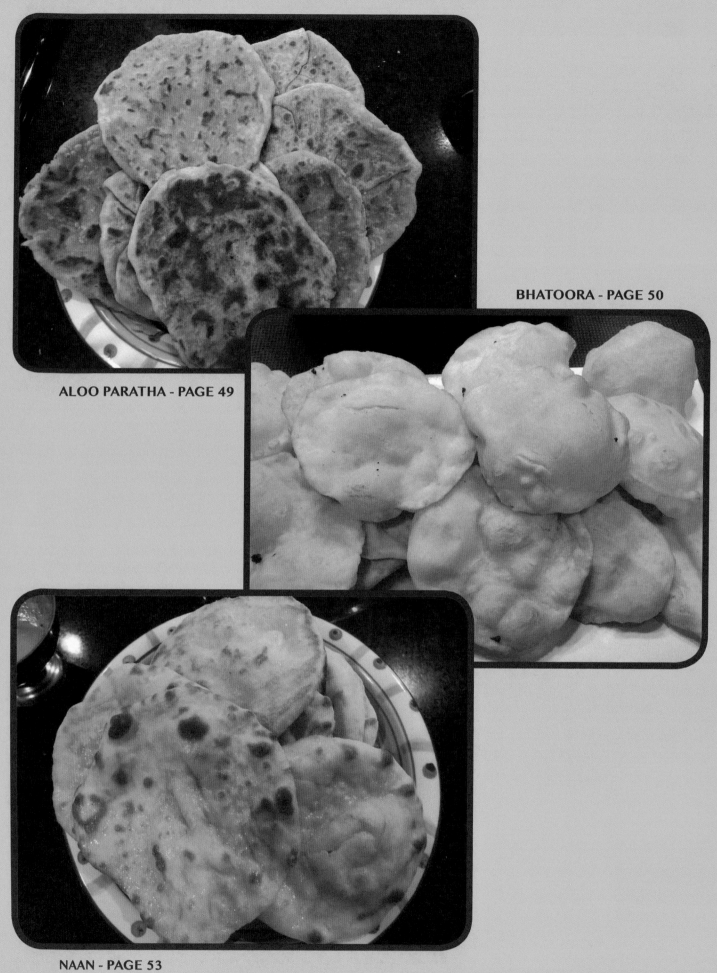

BHATOORA - PAGE 50

ALOO PARATHA - PAGE 49

NAAN - PAGE 53

CHAPTER 2: BREADS

Indian breads are made out of whole wheat flour or all purpose flour. They are served with vegetables, lentils and meat dishes. Plain bread is known as chapati and paratha. Fried breads are known as poori and bhatoora. Stuffed bread can be made with a stuffing of potatoes, cauliflowers, cabbage, etc. Masala breads are made by mixing vegetables and spices in the dough and then pan frying. Baked bread, known as naan, is the bread typically served in Indian restaurants.

The amount of water needed make the dough varies based on the type of grain and the age of the flour. The amount given in each recipe is a starting point, so add or reduce water to get the right consistency.

Chapati

Serves 8
Preparation time: 25 minutes
Cooking time: 30 minutes

Vegetarian

Vegan

Basic Indian roasted bread, served with many different dishes in this book.

Calories 150 • Calories from Fat 45 • Total Fat 5g • Cholesterol 0mg • Sodium 75mg • Total Carbohydrates 11g (Dietary Fiber 2g, Sugars 0g) • Protein 2g

Ingredients

2 cups ....whole wheat flour

2 T.. oil

½ t.. salt

¾ cup ....water (as needed)

• • •

¼ cup ....all purpose flour for rolling chapatis

2T................................. butter or ghee (optional)

Method

1. Combine all the ingredients in a mixing bowl and prepare dough that is soft but not sticky for rolling out chapatis. Cover and set aside for at least 20 minutes.

2. Knead dough for 2-3 minutes then separate dough into 16 equal parts. Using one part of dough, form a smooth ball in palm of your hands, press it down on a floured surface and roll into 6-7" rounds with a rolling pin. Sprinkle flour as needed to prevent chapati from sticking.

3. Heat a flat griddle on medium heat. Cook the chapati on one side until you see raised bubbles and then flip it over to cook the other side.

4. Lift the chapati with metal tongs and move the griddle to an off burner. Place the chapati directly over the flame (turn flame to high), until it puffs up. Turn the chapati on the other side to puff up more. Allow a few seconds on each side.

5. Turn heat to medium when done puffing.

6. Place the chapati on a plate and apply ghee or butter to the top side. Stack chapatis on top of each other as you make more.

Aloo Paratha

Vegetarian

Vegan

Serves 12
Preparation time: 30 minutes
Cooking time: 30 minutes

Calories 140 • Calories from Fat 25 • Total Fat 3g (Saturated Fat 0g, Trans Fat 0g) • Cholesterol 0mg • Sodium 390mg • Total Carbohydrates 25g (Dietary Fiber 4g, Sugars 1g) • Protein 4g

Ingredients

1 lb.. russet potatoes
(approx 2 cups of mashed potatoes)

• • •

Chapati dough

2 cups ....whole wheat flour
2 T... oil
½ t... salt
¾ cup .... water (as needed)

• • •

Potato stuffing

1 cup.. green peas
¼ cup each..................... finely chopped cilantro, ginger & jalapeno
1 t ....garam masala
2 T...................................... lime or lemon juice
1½ t.. salt

• • •

¼ cup .... oil for pan frying
¼ cup ....all purpose flour for rolling chapatis

Method

1. Boil potatoes in 4 cups of water for 20-30 minutes or until cooked. After they finish cooking, run them under cold running water to stop the cooking process. Then peel and mash smooth with a potato masher.

2. While potatoes are cooking:
   • Combine all ingredients in a mixing bowl and prepare dough that is soft but not sticky. Cover and set aside for at least 20 minutes.
   • Bring 1 cup of water to boil, add peas and cook for 3-4 minutes. Drain water completely and set aside.

3. Combine potatoes, boiled peas, and rest of the stuffing ingredients in a separate bowl.

4. Knead chapati dough for 2-3 minutes. Divide chapati dough and potato mixture into 12 equal parts.

5. Using one part of dough, form a smooth ball in palm of your hands. Press it down on a floured surface and roll into a 6-7" round with a rolling pin. Sprinkle flour as needed to prevent the chapati from sticking. Place one part potato mixture in the center of the chapati. Gather the dough from the edges and fold over to cover the stuffing. Pinch the dough together in the center to seal the paratha. Sprinkle all purpose flour and gently pat it down, then place the gathered side face down. Gently roll the paratha into 6" round with rolling pin. Roll all the parathas and arrange them on a cookie sheet.

6. Heat a flat griddle on medium heat. Cook the paratha on one side until you see raised bubbles and then flip it over to cook the other side. It will take about 1 minute on each side. Then apply ½ teaspoon of oil on one side, flip and apply ½ teaspoon of oil to the other side, and cook for about an additional 1 minute on each side until light brown. Line a serving plate with wax paper. Arrange parathas in a circle.

7. Enjoy with plain yogurt or cucumber raita (page 62).

Bhatoora

Vegetarian

Vegan

Serves 8
Preparation time: 30 minutes
Cooking time: 30 minutes

Calories 270 • Calories from Fat 160 • Total Fat 18g (Saturated Fat 2.5g, Trans Fat 0g) • Cholesterol 0mg • Sodium 290mg • Total Carbohydrates 24g (Dietary Fiber 1g, Sugars 0g) • Protein 3g

Ingredients

2 cups ....all purpose flour

2 T......................... yogurt or lemon or lime juice

3 T.. oil

½ t...baking soda

1 t .... salt

½ cup .... water (as needed)

• • •

¼ cup .... all purpose flour for rolling chapatis

• • •

Approx 2 cups of oil for deep frying

Method

Note: Bhatoora dough is semi-soft and requires less water than chapati dough.

1. Combine all the ingredients in a mixing bowl and prepare dough that is soft but not sticky for rolling out bhatooras. Cover and set aside for 30 minutes.

2. Knead dough for 2-3 minutes then divide dough into 24 equal parts. Roll into 3-4" rounds with a rolling pin on a lightly floured surface. If dough is nice and elastic you may not need to flour a surface. Roll all the bhatoora and arrange them on a cookie sheet.

3. Heat oil in frying pan on medium high (375°) heat.

4. Place bhatoora one at a time in the hot oil and pat it down with the back of a spatula, to encourage it to puff up. Once the bhatoora has puffed up and turned golden, flip it to cook the other side for 10-15 seconds. Then remove it from the oil and put it on a paper towel-lined plate to absorb the excess oil.

5. Serve hot with chole (page 92).

Poori

Serves 8
Preparation time: 30 minutes
Cooking time: 30 minutes

Vegetarian

Vegan

Calories 280 • Calories from Fat 180 • Total Fat 20g (Saturated Fat 3g, Trans Fat 0g) • Cholesterol 0mg • Sodium 150mg • Total Carbohydrates 22g (Dietary Fiber 3g, Sugars 0g) • Protein 4g

Ingredients

2 cups ....whole wheat flour

3 T.. oil

½ t... salt

½ cup ....water (as needed)

• • •

¼ cup ....all purpose flour for rolling chapatis

• • •

Approx 2 cup oil for deep frying

Method

Note: Poori dough is semi-soft and requires less water than chapati dough.

1 Combine all the ingredients in a mixing bowl and prepare semi-soft dough, the consistency of play dough. Cover and set aside for 30 minutes.

2 Knead dough for 2-3 minutes then divide it into 24 equal parts. Using one part of dough, form a smooth ball in palm of your hands. On a lightly floured surface roll into a 3-4" round with a rolling pin. Roll all the pooris and arrange them on a cookie sheet.

3 Heat oil in frying pan on medium high (375°) heat.

4 Place pooris one at a time in the hot oil and pat it down with the back of a spatula, to encourage it to puff up. Once the poori has puffed up and has a few brown spots, flip it to cook the other side for 10-15 seconds. Then remove it from the oil and put it on a paper towel-lined plate to absorb the excess oil.

5 Basic Indian fried bread and served with many different dishes in this book.

Masala Poori

Vegetarian

Vegan

Serves 8
Preparation time: 30 minutes
Cooking time: 30 minutes

Calories 290 • Calories from Fat 200 • Total Fat 22g (Saturated Fat 3g, Trans Fat 0g) • Cholesterol 0mg • Sodium 440mg • Total Carbohydrates 22g (Dietary Fiber 3g, Sugars 0g) • Protein 4g

Ingredients

2 cups	whole wheat flour
3 T	oil
½	salt
½ cup	water (as needed)
1 t	red chili powder
½ t	turmeric
1 t	black pepper
½ t	roasted cumin powder
½ t	ajwain

• • •

¼ cup .... all purpose flour for rolling chapatis

• • •

Approximately 2 cups of oil for deep frying

Method

Note: Poori dough is semi-soft and requires less water than chapati dough.

1. Combine all the ingredients in a mixing bowl and prepare semi-soft dough. Cover and set aside for 30 minutes.

2. Knead dough for 2-3 minutes then divide it into 24 equal parts. Using one part of dough, form a smooth ball in palm of your hands. On a lightly floured surface roll into a 3-4" round with a rolling pin.

3. Heat oil in frying pan on medium high (375°) heat.

4. Place masala pooris one at a time in the hot oil and pat it down with the back of a spatula, to encourage it to puff up. Once the poori has puffed up and has few brown spots, flip it to cook the other side for 10-15 seconds. Then remove it from the oil and put it on a paper towel-lined plate to absorb the excess oil.

5. Serve hot with yogurt or just enjoy it on its own.

Naan

Vegetarian

This is your basic Naan, similar to what is typically served as Indian restaurants.

Serves 8
Preparation time: 45 minutes
Cooking time: 30 minutes

Calories 220 • Calories from Fat 100 • Total Fat 11g (Saturated Fat 3g, Trans Fat 0g) • Cholesterol 10mg • Sodium 390mg • Total Carbohydrates 25g (Dietary Fiber 1g, Sugars 1g) • Protein 4g • 0.5 g omega-3 fatty acid

Ingredients

2 t ....yeast
1 T.. sugar
½ cup ....warm water
2 cups ....all purpose flour
1 t .... salt
3 T... oil
1 T... yogurt

• • •

2 T........................... butter for garnish (optional)

• • •

¼ cup ....all purpose flour for rolling naans

• • •

Pizza stone or cookie tray lined with aluminum foil for baking naan

Method

Note: Naan dough should be soft but not sticky – similar to chapati dough.

1. In a food processor or a bowl, combine the dry yeast and sugar. Add warm water and mix until yeast has dissolved. Cover and leave for 10 minutes or until the yeast is activated.

2. Prepare dough:
   - If using a food processor:
     Combine all the dough ingredients and mix with the kneading blade. Cover with a moist cloth and set aside for at least 30 minutes at room temperature or until the dough doubles in volume.
   - If mixing by hand:
     Mix all the dough ingredients in a bowl. Cover with a moist cloth and set aside for at least 30 minutes at room temperature or until the dough doubles in volume.

3. Preheat oven to 400°F. Move top rack in oven to the top and lay aluminum foil in a cookie tray and grease it gently. You can also use a pizza stone. While oven is preheating, leave the cookie tray or pizza stone in the oven to heat up.

4. Knead the dough for 2-3 minutes and separate in 8-10 equal parts. Using one part of dough form a smooth ball in palm of your hands. On a lightly floured surface roll into 7-8" rounds with a rolling pin. Roll out all the naans and place them on floured surface, cover them with a moist cloth.

5. Turn the oven to broil.

6. Place one or two naans on cookie sheet or pizza stone, making sure they are not touching. Cook for one minute. Watch the naan from the oven window while cooking. The naans will be puffy and lightly brown, with some brown spots. Remove from the oven and apply butter to one side.

7. Store in a foil-lined basket and cover with a napkin. Serve hot.

Garlic Naan

Vegetarian

Serves 8
Preparation time: 45 minutes
Cooking time: 30 minutes

Ingredients

2 t	yeast
1 T	sugar
¼ cup	warm water
2 cups	all purpose flour
1 ½ t	salt
3 T	oil
1 T	yogurt

¼ cup each	finely chopped garlic, onion, jalapeno & cilantro
1 T	lemon or lime juice

• • •

¼ cup	all purpose flour for rolling naans
2 T	butter for garnish (optional)

• • •

Pizza stone or cookie tray lined with aluminum foil for baking naan

Method

Note: Garlic naan dough should be drier than plain naan dough. Garlic, onion, jalapeno, and cilantro will add some moisture.

1. In a food processor or a bowl combine the dry yeast and sugar. Add warm water and mix until yeast has dissolved. Cover and leave for 10 minutes or until the yeast is activated.

2. Prepare dough:
   - If using a food processor:
   Combine all the dough ingredients and mix with the kneading blade. Cover with a moist cloth and set aside for at least 30 minutes at room temperature or until the dough doubles in volume.
   - If mixing by hand:
   Mix all the dough ingredients in a bowl. Cover with a moist cloth and set aside for at least 30 minutes at room temperature or until the dough doubles in volume.

3. Preheat oven to 400°F. Move top rack in oven to the top and lay aluminum foil in a cookie tray and grease it gently. You can also use a pizza stone. While oven is preheating, leave the cookie tray or pizza stone in the oven to heat up.

4. Knead the dough for 2-3 minutes and separate in 8-10 equal parts. Using one part of dough form a smooth ball in palm of your hands. On a lightly floured surface, roll into 7-8" rounds with a rolling pin. Roll out all the naans and place them on floured surface, cover them with a moist cloth.

5. Turn the oven to broil.

6. Place one or two naans on cookie sheet or pizza stone, making sure they are not touching. Cook for one minute. Watch the naan from the oven window while cooking. The naans will be puffy and lightly brown, with some brown spots. Remove from the oven and apply butter to one side.

7. Store in a foil-lined basket and cover with a napkin. Serve hot.

Paratha

Vegetarian

Vegan

Chapatis and parathas are basic Indian breads.

Serves 8
Preparation time: 35 minutes
Cooking time: 20 minutes

Calories 160 • Calories from Fat 70 • Total Fat 8g (Saturated Fat 0.5g, Trans Fat 0g) • Cholesterol 0mg • Sodium 150mg • Total Carbohydrates 22g (Dietary Fiber 3g, Sugars 0g) • Protein 4g • 0.5 g omega-3 fatty acid

Ingredients

2 cups ....whole wheat flour	
4 T... oil	2 T .... oil
1 t .... salt	¼ cup ....all purpose flour for rolling chapatis
½ cup ....water (as needed)	

• • •

Method

Note: Plain paratha dough is semi-soft and requires less water compared to chapati dough.

1. Combine all the dough ingredients in a mixing bowl and prepare dough that is soft but not sticky. Cover and set aside for 30 minutes.

2. Divide dough into 8 equal parts.

3. Flour a clean work surface and roll 3-4" rounds with a rolling pin. Apply some oil using a pastry brush. Fold it in half and then half again. Sprinkle some flour and roll into a 6-7" round.

4. Heat a griddle on medium heat. Transfer the paratha to the griddle and cook it on both sides until the surface starts to bubble. Spread ½ teaspoon of oil on each side and continue to cook until brown spots appear.

Vegetable Paratha

Vegetarian

Vegan

Serves 8
Preparation time: 30 minutes
Cooking time: 30 minutes

Calories 200 • Calories from Fat 70 • Total Fat 8g (Saturated Fat 1g, Trans Fat 0g) • Cholesterol 0mg • Sodium 20mg • Total Carbohydrates 29g (Dietary Fiber 4g, Sugars 7g) • Protein 5g • 0.5 g omega-3 fatty acid

Ingredients

2 cups	whole wheat flour
4 T	oil
½ cup each	finely chopped spinach/ methi bhaji, scallion, & cabbage
1 T	finely chopped garlic
2 t	salt
½ t	turmeric

1 t	red chili powder
½ t	ground black pepper
3 T	sugar (optional)
¾ cup	yogurt

(Substitute 3 T lemon/lime juice to make vegan)

• • •

¼ cup	oil
¼ cup	all purpose flour for rolling chapatis

Method

Note: Masala paratha dough should be drier compared to plain paratha dough. Spinach, scallion, cabbage, garlic, and yogurt will add some moisture.

1. Combine all the ingredients in a mixing bowl and prepare dough that is soft but not sticky. Cover and set aside for 30 minutes.

2. Divide dough in 16 equal parts. Heat a flat pan on medium heat.

3. Flour a clean work surface and roll each part into a 6-7" round with a rolling pin. Transfer the paratha to the griddle and roast it on both sides until it starts showing bubbles. Grease the parathas with ½ teaspoon oil on each side until brown spots appear.

4. Enjoy with yogurt or by itself. You can prepare them ahead of time and reheat it in toaster oven for 2-3 minutes or 20 seconds in the microwave.

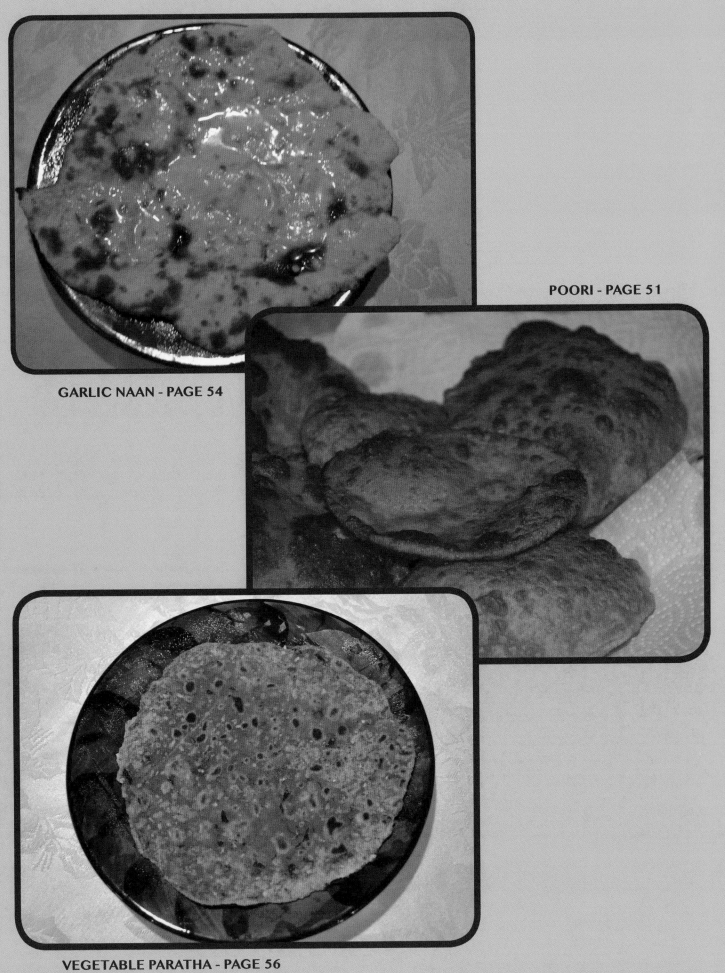

GARLIC NAAN - PAGE 54

POORI - PAGE 51

VEGETABLE PARATHA - PAGE 56

COCONUT CHUTNEY - PAGE 60

CUCUMBER RAITA - PAGE 62

TOMATO & ONION SALAD - PAGE 65

CILANTRO CHUTNEY - PAGE 60

CHAPTER 3: CONDIMENTS & SALADS

Condiments and salads are part of every meal. Chutneys are normally a combination of spices, vegetables, and/or fruit. Chutneys are used as dips for pakodas. Raita is made with yogurt and used as sauce, dip, or side dish. Yogurt raita goes really well with spicy food. Bean salads are a perfect choice for a meal on a hot summer day.

Cilantro Chutney

Serves 12

Vegan
Vegetarian
Gluten Free

Serve with pakodas or other fried appetizers.

Calories 20 • Calories from Fat 15 • Total Fat 1.5g (Saturated Fat 0g, Trans Fat 0g) • Cholesterol 0mg • Sodium 100mg • Total Carbohydrates 1g (Dietary Fiber 0g, Sugars 0g) • Protein 1g

Ingredients

2 cups ....chopped cilantro	½ t.. salt
¼ cup .... blanched peanuts	2 T.. lime or lemon juice
¼ cup .... chopped jalapeno	½ cup ....water

Method

1. Combine all ingredients in a blender. Blend for 3-4 minutes until it forms a smooth, thick paste. Add an additional 1-2 tablespoons of water at a time as needed to help with the blending.

Coconut Chutney

Serves 12

Vegan
Vegetarian
Gluten Free

Serve with daal dosa, mendu wada, rawa idli, rawa dosa or upma.

Calories 80 • Calories from Fat 50 • Total Fat 6g (Saturated Fat 4.5g, Trans Fat 0g) • Cholesterol 5mg • Sodium 100mg • Total Carbohydrates 7g (Dietary Fiber 3g, Sugars 1g) • Protein 2g

Ingredients

1 cup...................... unsweetened grated coconut	1 T..butter or oil
½ cup .... daalia	2 T..urad daal
½ t... salt	¼ t.. cumin seeds
2 T..................................... lime or lemon juice	¼ t...mustard seeds
¾ cup ....water	1/8 t.. asafetida
• • •	4 to 6 leaves ....limdo/curry leaves

Method

1. Combine coconut, daalia, salt, lime or lemon juice, and water in a blender. Blend on high speed to form a nice thick paste. Add an additional 1-2 tablespoons of water at a time as needed. Transfer to a bowl.

2. Heat butter or oil in a small pan. Add urad daal, cumin, and mustard seeds. When mustard seeds crackle and the cumin and urad daal turn brown, add the asafetida and limdo/curry leaves. Pour it over the coconut chutney mixture and stir in well.

Sweet Chutney

Vegan

Vegetarian

Gluten Free

Chutney with Apples:
Calories 80 • Calories from Fat 0 • Total Fat 0g (Saturated Fat 0g, Trans Fat 0g) • Cholesterol 0mg • Sodium 105mg • Total Carbohydrates 19g (Dietary Fiber 0g, Sugars 17g) • Protein 0g

Ingredients - Apple

1 cup	apple butter
½ cup	brown sugar
3 T	lime or lemon juice
½ T	roasted cumin powder (page 20)
½ t	red chili powder
½ t	salt
¾ cup	water

Chutney with Dates:
Calories 60 • Calories from Fat 0 • Total Fat 0g (Saturated Fat 0g, Trans Fat 0g) • Cholesterol 0mg • Sodium 105mg • Total Carbohydrates 16g (Dietary Fiber 1g, Sugars 15g) • Protein 0g

Ingredients - Dates

1 cup	cooked & pureed dates
3 T	dried mango powder
½ cup	brown sugar or jaggery
½ T	roasted cumin powder (page 20)
½ t	chili powder
½ t	salt
¾ cup	water

Chutney with Tamarind:
Calories 90 • Calories from Fat 0 • Total Fat 0g (Saturated Fat 0g, Trans Fat 0g) • Cholesterol 0mg • Sodium 105mg • Total Carbohydrates 24g (Dietary Fiber 1g, Sugars 24g) • Protein 0g

Ingredients - Tamarind

1 cup	tamarind paste
1 cup	brown sugar or jaggery
½ T	roasted cumin powder (page 20)
½ t	chili powder
½ t	salt
¾ cup	water

Method

1. Combine all the ingredients in a blender. Blend for 3-4 minutes until it forms a thick paste and then add enough additional water to yield approximately 2 cups of chutney.

Boondi Raita

Serves 8

Vegetarian

Gluten Free

Boondi is made from chickpea/besan flour. You can buy boondi at any Indian grocery store.

Calories 70 • Calories from Fat 10 • Total Fat 1g (Saturated Fat 0.5g, Trans Fat 0g) • Cholesterol 5mg • Sodium 125mg • Total Carbohydrates 10g (Dietary Fiber 1g, Sugars 5g) • Protein 5g

Ingredients

1 cup.....................boondi	¼ t.....................red chili powder
2 cup..................... yogurt	2 T.....................chopped cilantro
¼ t..................... salt	¼ t..................... black pepper

Method

1. Combine all the ingredients in a bowl, mix well, and serve right away.

Cucumber Raita

Serves 12

Vegetarian

Gluten Free

Calories 30 • Calories from Fat 5 • Total Fat 0.5g (Saturated Fat 0g, Trans Fat 0g) • Cholesterol 0mg • Sodium 30mg • Total Carbohydrates 4g (Dietary Fiber 0g, Sugars 4g) • Protein 2g

Ingredients

2 cups ....plain yogurt	1 t..................... sugar
1 cup..................... peeled & grated cucumber (squeeze out extra liquid)	½ t.....................roasted ground cumin (page 20)
	½ t..................... salt
¼ cup .... chopped scallions	½ t..................... black pepper
1 cup..................... finely chopped tomato	2 T.....................chopped cilantro for garnish

Method

1. Combine all the ingredients in a bowl and mix well. Garnish with cilantro. Refrigerate for 30 minutes before serving.

Potato Raita

Serves 12

Vegetarian

Gluten Free

Makes a good side dish with any meal.

Calories 40 • Calories from Fat 5 • Total Fat 0.5g (Saturated Fat 0g, Trans Fat 0g) • Cholesterol 0mg • Sodium 30mg • Total Carbohydrates 6g (Dietary Fiber 0g, Sugars 3g) • Protein 2g

Ingredients

1 cup or ½ lb .... russet potatoes	¼ t .... red chili powder
½ cup .... finely chopped tomatoes	¼ t .... salt
2 cups .... yogurt	2 T .... chopped cilantro

Method

1. Boil potatoes in 2 cups of water for 20-30 minutes, until soft. After they finish cooking, run them under cold running water to halt the cooking process, then peel and dice into ¼" pieces.

2. Combine all the ingredients in a bowl and mix well. Chill for at least one hour.

Chickpea Salad

Serves 12

Vegan

Vegetarian

Gluten Free

Enjoy as a meal by itself or as a side dish.

Calories 80 • Calories from Fat 10 • Total Fat 1g (Saturated Fat 0g, Trans Fat 0g) • Cholesterol 0mg • Sodium 105mg • Total Carbohydrates 15g (Dietary Fiber 3g, Sugars 3g) • Protein 3g

Ingredients

2 cups .... cooked chickpeas	¼ cup .... finely chopped cilantro
1 cup or ½ lb .... russet potatoes boiled & cubed	½ t .... salt
	½ t .... crushed black pepper
• • •	½ t .... red chili powder
1 cup .... finely chopped tomatoes	2 T .... lime or lemon juice
½ cup each .... finely chopped onion, cucumber, bell pepper, & carrot	2 T .... chaat masala

Method

1. Boil potatoes in 2 cups of water for 20-30 minutes, until soft. After they finish cooking, run them under cold running water to halt the cooking process, then peel and dice into ¼" pieces.

2. Combine all the ingredients in a bowl and mix well. Chill for an hour.

Moong Bean Salad

Vegan

Vegetarian

Gluten Free

Calories 50 • Calories from Fat 5 • Total Fat 0.5g (Saturated Fat 0.5g, Trans Fat 0g) • Cholesterol 0mg • Sodium 610mg • Total Carbohydrates 11g (Dietary Fiber 3g, Sugars 6g) • Protein 3g • 120% Vitamin A, 50% vitamin C

Ingredients

2 cups .... sprouted moong beans (page 20)

• • •

1 cup each .... finely chopped tomato, cucumber, & carrot

½ cup each .... finely chopped, green pepper, & onion

¼ cup .... finely chopped cilantro

1 t .... salt

½ t each .... crushed black pepper, red chili powder, & black pepper

2 T .... lime or lemon juice

Method

1. Boil water and add sprouted moong beans. Once water starts boiling again, boil for 5 minutes on medium, then drain. Allow it to cool down.

2. Transfer sprouted moong beans to a bowl and combine with the remaining ingredients. Mix well and chill for at least an hour.

3. Enjoy as a meal or side dish.

Tomato & Onion Salad

Serves 8

Vegan

Vegetarian

Gluten Free

THis a basic salad, served with almost every Indian meal.

Calories 15 • Calories from Fat 0 • Total Fat 0g (Saturated Fat 0g, Trans Fat 0g) • Cholesterol 0mg • Sodium 75mg • Total Carbohydrates 4g (Dietary Fiber 1g, Sugars 2g) • Protein 1g

Ingredients

2 cups .... thinly sliced tomato

1 cup.......................................thinly sliced onion

1 cup...............................thinly sliced cucumber

¼ t.. salt

¼ t...crushed pepper

¼ t...red chili powder

2 T...chopped cilantro

2 t...lime or lemon juice

Method

1 Thinly slice tomato, onion, and cucumbers. Toss with all of the spices. Chill for 30 minutes.

CHICKEN BIRYANI
- PAGE 70

TANDOORI CHICKEN
- PAGE 81

KHEEMA - PAGE 75

CHAPTER 4: MEAT MAIN DISHES

Curries, as well as dry preparations of meats, are prevalent in North Indian cuisine. The Mughal invasion in 16th century had a major influence on the preparation of Tandoori dishes. Chicken, lamb, and goat is used in many dishes. The coastal region consumed lots of fish. Meats are typically marinated for flavor and tenderness.

Butter Chicken

Gluten free

Serves 8
Preparation time: 30 minutes
Cooking time: 20 minutes

Calories 170 • Calories from Fat 90 • Total Fat 10g (Saturated Fat 5g, Trans Fat 0g) • Cholesterol 55mg • Sodium 530mg • Total Carbohydrates 4g (Dietary Fiber 1g, Sugars 2g) • Protein 13g • 20% vitamin C

Ingredients

Marinade

¼ cup each ....finely chopped garlic, ginger, & jalapeno
1 t each .... red chili powder, garam masala, & crushed black pepper
2 T............................... lime or lemon juice
2 T.. oil
1 t .... salt
1 lb.....................boneless skinless chicken cut into 1" cubes

¼ cup ....water
• • •
¼ cup .... butter
1 t .... cumin seeds
1 t ....red chili powder
1 cup..tomato sauce
• • •
½ cup .... sour cream
¼ cup .... finely chopped cilantro
1 t ....roasted cumin powder (page 20)

Method

1. Combine all the ingredients for the marinade in a blender or food processor. Add ¼ cup of water as needed. Transfer the marinade to a glass bowl and add the chicken pieces.

2. Cover and refrigerate for at least 4 hours.

3. Heat butter in a heavy pot on medium heat. When the butter is melted add cumin seeds and once they turn dark brown, add chili powder and tomato sauce. Cook for 1-2 minutes. This will give the dish a nice red color.

4. Adjust heat to high and add the chicken and all of the marinade. Once it starts to simmer, reduce the heat to medium, cover, and simmer for 5-7 more minutes or until the chicken is cooked through. Stir occasionally to prevent it from sticking.

5. Transfer the cooked chicken to a serving dish. Add sour cream and mix well. Sprinkle with cilantro and roasted jeera powder.

6. Serve with jeera rice (page 100) or plain basmati rice.

Chicken Cutlets

Serves 6
Preparation time: 20 minutes
Cooking time: 20 minutes

Calories 190 • Calories from Fat 80 • Total Fat 9g (Saturated Fat 1.5g, Trans Fat 0g) • Cholesterol 110mg • Sodium 370mg • Total Carbohydrates 6g (Dietary Fiber 1g, Sugars 2g) • Protein 19g

Ingredients

1 lb.....................boneless skinless chicken breast
cut into 3x3" and about ½" thick pieces

• • •

Paste
2 T each .... finely chopped garlic & ginger
1 t .... red chili powder

½ t.. salt

• • •

2 .... eggs
½ cup .... bread crumbs
¼ cup .... oil for frying

Method

1. Pat the chicken pieces dry with paper towels.

2. Combine finely chopped garlic, ginger, red chili powder, and salt in a mini food processor and make into a paste. Add 1 to 2 tablespoons of water as needed. Transfer paste to a bowl and apply the paste to both sides of the chicken pieces.

3. Cover and refrigerate for at least 30 minutes.

4. Lightly beat the eggs. Dip one piece of chicken at a time into the beaten eggs and then roll it in a plate of bread crumbs.

5. Heat 2 tablespoons of oil in a heavy skillet or griddle on medium to high heat. Cook chicken on both sides until nice and brown, about 2-3 minutes on each side. Cover the skillet or griddle with a lid and cook for 3-4 minutes or until the chicken is done.

6. Serve with cilantro chutney (page 60).

Chicken Biryani

Gluten Free

Serves 12
Preparation time: 45 minutes
Cooking time: 1 hour 15 minutes

Calories 270 • Calories from Fat 130 • Total Fat 14g (Saturated Fat 4g, Trans Fat 0g) • Cholesterol 10mg • Sodium 600mg • Total Carbohydrates 32g (Dietary Fiber 2g, Sugars 3g) • Protein 4g • 30% vitamin C

This is one of my favorite recipes so, although the list of ingredients and process can seem overwhelming, I encourage you to give it a try, as it is absolutely worth the effort and time. I've given instructions in steps that you can follow, one at a time, setting different preparations aside so that you can put them all together at the end. As with all recipes, read through it carefully before you begin and assemble all the ingredients. A good biryani is a pleasure to behold and eat! Make extra (this recipe serves 12) and enjoy it the next day. Special thanks to Manijeh DaVitre for sharing this recipe.

Ingredients - Part 1

½ cup .... oil
2 cups .... caramelized onions (page 18)

2 cups .... basmati rice
15-20 strands........................... saffron + 2 T milk

Method - Part 1

1. Caramelizing of the onion gives the gravy a rich flavor and brown color. Keep ¼ cup of caramelized onion aside for garnish, use the rest in the biryani paste.

2. Wash and drain rice, then soak in 4 cups of water.

3. Prepare saffron (page 20)

Ingredients - Part 2

5 T..biryani masala
¼ cup each........... finely chopped garlic & ginger
• • •
¼ cup each...................... sliced almonds, raisins, & cashew pieces
2 lb.................. chicken drumstick or thigh meat, cut into bite-size pieces

• • •
5 pieces .... bay leaves
10 pieces .... cloves
2 cups each .... potatoes & tomatoes cut into big pieces
1 t .... salt
½ cup .... yogurt

Method - Part 2

1. Combine in a blender or food processor biryani masala, garlic, ginger, caramelized onion, and ½ cup of water to make a biryani paste. Keep paste aside.

2. Heat ½ cup of oil in a 6 quart heavy-bottomed pot, add almonds and cashews, and cook until edges turn brown, then set aside.

Method - Part 2 (continued)

3 Add raisins and cook until they puff up, then set those aside as well.

4 Add chicken thigh or drumsticks and cook for 3-4 minutes on high heat until edges turn brown, then set aside.

5 In the remaining oil, add bay leaves, cloves, and biryani paste and cook for 3-4 minutes on medium heat.

6 Add potatoes and cook for 4-5 minutes. Add tomatoes and cook for an additional 4-5 minutes.

7 Add 1 teaspoon salt, precooked chicken, and yogurt. After it starts bubbling, cover and simmer for 20-25 minutes.

Ingredients - Part 3

2 t .... salt	¼ cup .... finely chopped cilantro
¼ cup .... butter	¼ cup .... finely chopped mint
¼ cup .... lime or lemon juice	¼ cup .... caramelized onion
½ cup .... milk	(prepared in Step 1)

Method - Part 3

PREHEAT OVEN TO 350°F

1 While mixture is simmering, start preparing rice. Boil 4 cups of water. Drain the soaked rice and add it to the boiling water. Add 2 teaspoons of salt and boil for 5-6 minutes uncovered. Drain any remaining water from the rice.

2 Once chicken is ready, add rice on top of chicken. Cut ¼ cup of butter into small pieces and dot the top of the rice. Drizzle ¼ cup lemon or lime juice on top of the rice. Add ¼ cup of milk to saffron mixture and drizzle on top of rice. Drizzle an additional ¼ cup of milk over the top of the rice. DO NOT STIR.

3 Cover the pot with aluminum foil and place the lid on top. Bake in the oven for 30 minutes.

4 After removing the biryani from the oven, add cilantro, mint, and caramelized onion. Toss gently and transfer it to a serving dish. Decorate with almonds, cashews and raisins.

5 Serve with yogurt or cucumber raita (page 62) and papadam.

Chicken Tikka

Gluten Free

Serves 8
Preparation time: 30 minutes
Cooking time: 30 minutes

Calories 180 • Calories from Fat 110 • Total Fat 12g (Saturated Fat 2.5g, Trans Fat 0g) • Cholesterol 35mg • Sodium 190mg • Total Carbohydrates 5g (Dietary Fiber 1g, Sugars 2g) • Protein 13g

Ingredients

Marinade

2 T	white vinegar
½ t	salt
3 T each	finely chopped garlic & ginger
2 T	lime or lemon juice
½ cup	finely chopped cilantro
1 t	garam masala
1 t	red chili powder
1 t	turmeric
4 T	olive oil
½ cup	yogurt

• • •

Cut into 1" cubes for skewers

1 lb	boneless skinless chicken breast
1 cup	red onion
1 cup	cherry tomato

• • •

Garnish

1 cup	onion cut into rings
1 whole	lime or lemon cut into wedges
2 t	chaat masala

Method

Note: If you are using wooden skewers, soak in water for at least 30 minutes prior to cooking to prevent them from burning.

1. Combine all the ingredients for the marinade in a blender or food processor. Transfer marinade to a glass bowl and add chicken pieces, stirring to coat.

2. Cover and refrigerate for at least 4-6 hours.

3. Light the grill and leave it on high for direct heat grilling.

4. Thread the chicken onto skewers, alternating with red onion and cherry tomato.

5. Cooking the skewers:
   - If using a barbecue grill:
     Place skewers on the skewer rack on the hottest part of the grill. Cook for 3-4 minutes, turn skewers, apply some marinade with pastry brush, and cook until done. It will be charred on edges.
   - If using an oven:
     Preheat oven to broil. Arrange skewers on an oven safe tray in a single layer on top rack and bake for 10-15 minutes or until cooked through, turning after 5-7 minutes.

6. Arrange jeera rice (page 100), onion rings, and lime or lemon wedges on a platter. Add skewers on top and sprinkle with chaat masala before serving.

Chicken Vindaloo

Gluten free

Serves 8
Preparation time: 30 minutes
Cooking time: 45 minutes

Calories 230 • Calories from Fat 140 • Total Fat 15g (Saturated Fat 2.5g, Trans Fat 0g) • Cholesterol 40mg • Sodium 490mg • Total Carbohydrates 10g (Dietary Fiber 1g, Sugars 4g) • Protein 14g • 30% vitamin C

Ingredients

2 cups .... caramelized onions (page 18)

• • •

Vindaloo paste

2 T .... garam masala

¼ cup .... white wine vinegar

1 t .... red chili powder

½ t .... black pepper

1 T .... light brown sugar

¼ cup .... water

• • •

¼ cup .... vegetable oil

¼ cup .... finely chopped ginger

¼ cup .... finely chopped garlic

1 T .... coriander powder

1 t .... turmeric

1 lb .... boneless skinless chicken breast cut bite size pieces

1 cup .... tomato sauce

1 cup .... peeled & quartered potatoes

1 t .... salt

Method

1. Combine all the ingredients for the paste plus the caramelized onions in a blender or food processor. Add water as needed to make the paste blend smoothly.

2. Heat 4 tablespoons of oil in a heavy-bottomed pot, add ginger and garlic, and cook for 2-3 minutes. Add coriander powder and turmeric. Cook for additional 1-2 minutes. Add the chicken pieces and brown lightly on each side. Add the vindaloo paste, tomato sauce, potatoes, and salt. Stir to combine and then bring to a boil. Cover and simmer for about 30-40 minutes. Stir occasionally to prevent sticking.

3. Serve with jeera rice (page 100) or plain basmati rice.

Goan Shrimp Curry

Gluten Free

Serves 8
Preparation time: 25 minutes
Cooking time: 20 minutes

Calories 120 • Calories from Fat 50 • Total Fat 6g (Saturated Fat 1g, Trans Fat 0g) • Cholesterol 100mg • Sodium 640mg • Total Carbohydrates 4g (Dietary Fiber 1g, Sugars 2g) • Protein 11g

Ingredients

Gravy

3 whole	red chilies
¼ cup	vinegar
2 T	unsweetened shredded coconut
1 cup	chopped tomatoes
¼ cup	finely chopped jalapeno
4 whole	uncooked peeled & deveined shrimp – remove tail
1 cup	finely chopped onion
¼ cup	finely chopped ginger
¼ cup	finely chopped garlic
2 t	garam masala
1 t	turmeric
3 T	coriander powder
½ t	crushed black pepper
¼ cup	water (as needed)

• • •

¼ cup	oil
1 t	cumin seeds
½ t	mustard seeds
4 whole	bay leaves
1 t	salt
2 lb	uncooked peeled & deveined shrimp

Method

1. Combine all the ingredients for the gravy in a blender or food processor. Add water as needed.

2. Heat ¼ cup of oil in a heavy pot on medium heat. Add mustard and cumin seeds. When mustard seeds crackle and the cumin seeds turn brown, add bay leaves. Add gravy to the pot and cook for 10-12 minutes, then add salt and shrimp, and cook just until they turn pink. Allow about 3-4 minutes.

3. Serve with jeera rice (page 100) or plain basmati rice.

Kheema

Gluten Free

Serves 6
Preparation time: 20 minutes
Cooking time: 20 minutes

Calories 220 • Calories from Fat 120 • Total Fat 13g (Saturated Fat 5g, Trans Fat 0g) • Cholesterol 50mg • Sodium 450mg • Total Carbohydrates 9g (Dietary Fiber 2g, Sugars 3g) • Protein 15g • 15% vitamin A, 20% vitamin C

Ingredients

1 lb	ground lamb or turkey or beef
1 cup	finely chopped onion
¼ cup	finely chopped garlic
½ cup	finely chopped tomatoes
2 T	finely chopped jalapeno
1 t	garam masala
1 t	lime or lemon juice
1 cup	green peas
1 t	salt
½ cup	water (as needed)

Method

1. Cook ground meat in a heavy pot until evenly browned. While cooking, break the meat apart with a wooden spoon until crumbled. Transfer cooked meat to a bowl and drain off all but approximately 1 tablespoon fat.

2. Cook onion in that fat for 4-5 minutes. Add garlic and cook for 1-2 minutes. Add tomatoes and cook for 3-4 minutes. Add jalapeno and garam masala and cook for 2-3 minutes. Return the browned meat to the pot and add lime or lemon juice, green peas, salt, and ¼ cup of water. Reduce heat to low and simmer for 10 to 15 minutes or until meat is fully cooked. Mixture should be moist. If it is too dry, add 2-3 tablespoons of water and cook for an additional 1-2 minutes.

3. Serve with jeera rice (page 100) or plain basmati rice.

BUTTER CHICKEN - PAGE 68

CHICKEN VINDALOO - PAGE 73

GOAN SHRIMP CURRY - PAGE 74

MASALA CHICKEN CURRY
- PAGE 78

Lamb Meatballs

Gluten Free

Serves 8
Preparation time: 20 minutes
Cooking time: 20 minutes

Calories 210 • Calories from Fat 150 • Total Fat 17g (Saturated Fat 6g, Trans Fat 0g) • Cholesterol 40mg • Sodium 200mg • Total Carbohydrates 4g (Dietary Fiber 1g, Sugars 2g) • Protein 10g

Ingredients

1 lb	ground lamb
2 T	finely chopped garlic
2 T	finely chopped ginger
3 T	finely chopped green chilies
1 t	garam masala
¼ cup	besan
1 t	coriander powder

1 t	red chili powder
½ t	salt

• • •

1 t	chaat masala
1 whole	lime or lemon cut into wedges
¼ cup	oil

Method

1. Combine ground lamb, finely chopped garlic, ginger, green chilies, garam masala, besan, coriander powder, red chili powder, and salt. Divide into 24 parts. Roll each piece into a ball with your hands.

2. Steam meatballs in a vegetable steamer for 20 minutes, until the center is no longer pink. Heat 2 tablespoons of oil in a heavy pot and pan fry the meatballs on medium until they brown, about 5-7 minutes. Transfer to a dish on paper towels. Sprinkle chaat masala.

3. Serve with lime or lemon wedges and cilantro chutney (page 60).

Masala Chicken Curry

Serves 8
Preparation time: 20 minutes
Cooking time: 20 minutes

Calories 150 • Calories from Fat 80 • Total Fat 9g (Saturated Fat 1.5g, Trans Fat 0g) • Cholesterol 40mg • Sodium 460mg • Total Carbohydrates 4g (Dietary Fiber 1g, Sugars 2g) • Protein 15g

Ingredients

Marinade

¼ cup	yogurt
1 t	red chili powder
½ t	turmeric
1 t	salt

• • •

1 lb	chicken cut into 1" pieces

• • •

Gravy

1 cup	finely chopped onion
1 T	finely chopped ginger
1 T	finely chopped garlic

1 t	garam masala
1 cup	finely chopped tomato
¼ cup	cashew powder
2 T	coriander powder
½ t	black pepper

• • •

4 T	oil
1 t	cumin seeds
1 cup	chicken broth

• • •

¼ cup	finely chopped cilantro

Method

1. Combine all the ingredients for the marinade in a mixing bowl. Add chicken, stir to coat, and set aside for at least 20 minutes in the refrigerator.

2. Combine all the ingredients for the gravy in a blender or a food processor.

3. Heat 2 tablespoons of oil in a heavy pot on medium to high heat. Add cumin seeds, and once they turn dark brown, add the gravy and cook for another 5-6 minutes. Set aside.

4. Heat 2 tablespoons of oil in another heavy pot on medium to high heat. Add marinated chicken and cook on high heat for 4-5 minutes, or until the chicken is cooked through.

5. Combine chicken and gravy and cook for 3-4 minutes. Add 1 cup of chicken broth. Cover and simmer for 8-10 minutes.

6. Garnish with cilantro.

7. Serve with paratha (page 55), jeera rice (page 100), or plain basmati rice.

Masala Shrimp

Gluten Free

Serves 8
Preparation time: 20 minutes
Cooking time: 20 minutes

Calories 160 • Calories from Fat 110 • Total Fat 13g (Saturated Fat 1.5g, Trans Fat 0g) • Cholesterol 95mg • Sodium 1220mg • Total Carbohydrates 2g (Dietary Fiber 1g, Sugars 2g) • Protein 10g

Ingredients

Marinade

½ T..red chili powder
½ T...garam masala
2 T...garlic paste
2 T..ginger paste
1 t ....turmeric
3 T..coriander powder
½ t ....crushed black pepper
½ T... salt

• • •

1 lb............. uncooked peeled & deveined shrimp

• • •

¼ cup .... oil
½ t...cumin seeds

• • •

Garnish

¼ cup .... finely chopped cilantro
1 whole............... lime or lemon cut into wedges

Method

1 Combine all the ingredients for the marinade in a blender or food processor. Transfer to a glass bowl and add shrimp, stirring well to coat.

2 Cover and refrigerate for at least two hours.

3 Heat ¼ cup oil in a heavy pot on medium to high heat. Add cumin seeds, and once they turn dark brown, add the shrimp and the marinade. Cook for 4-5 minutes on medium to high heat, stirring constantly until the shrimp is just cooked.

4 In a serving dish, make a bed of jeera rice (page 100). Pour shrimp mixture on top and garnish with cilantro and lemon wedges. Can also be served with plain basmati rice.

Saag Chicken

Gluten Free

Serves 8
Preparation time: 30 minutes
Cooking time: 30 minutes

Calories 200 • Calories from Fat 110 • Total Fat 11g (Saturated Fat 3.5g, Trans Fat 0g) • Cholesterol 50mg • Sodium 590mg • Total Carbohydrates 11g (Dietary Fiber 4g, Sugars 2g) • Protein 16g • 45% vitamin A, 35% vitamin C, 15% iron

Ingredients

Marinade

¼ cup each	finely chopped garlic, ginger, & jalapeno
1 t	red chili powder
1 t	garam masala
1 t	salt

• • •

1 lb .... boneless/skinless chicken cut into 1" pieces

• • •

½ cup	water
⅛ t	baking soda
½ t	salt
1 lb	frozen chopped spinach or 8 cups of fresh chopped spinach

• • •

¼ cup	oil
1 cup	finely chopped onion
1 cup	finely chopped tomato
½ cup	sour cream

Method

1. Combine all the ingredients for marinade in a blender or a food processor. Transfer marinade to a glass bowl and add chicken, stirring to coat.

2. Cover and refrigerate for at least half an hour.

3. While chicken is marinating, combine ½ cup water, baking soda, salt, and spinach in a pot and cook for 7-8 minutes on medium heat, until the spinach is soft. Let it cool for 10 minutes, then puree. An immersion blender is recommended, however, a regular blender will also work, just be sure the spinach has sufficiently cooled.

4. Heat 3 tablespoons of oil in a heavy pot and add chopped onions and cook for 5-7 minutes. Add tomatoes and cook for 5-6 minutes. Add pureed spinach and cook for 5-6 minutes. Set aside.

5. Heat 3 tablespoons of oil in heavy pot and add chicken and marinade. Cook on medium to high heat until chicken is cooked through. Transfer chicken to spinach mixture and cook for 6-8 minutes on low heat. Cover and let it simmer for 5-7 minutes. Remove from heat.

6. Add ½ cup sour cream and mix well.

7. Serve with jeera rice (page 100), plain basmati rice, or paratha (page 55).

Tandoori Chicken

Gluten Free

Serves 12
Preparation time: 30 minutes
Cooking time: 30 minutes

Calories 80 • Calories from Fat 15• Total Fat 1.5g (Saturated Fat 0g, Trans Fat 0g) • Cholesterol 35mg • Sodium 230mg • Total Carbohydrates 4g (Dietary Fiber 1g, Sugars 2g) • Protein 13g • 40% vitamin C

Ingredients

2 lbs ....bone-in or boneless chicken, skinned (use legs, breasts, or a combination of two)
1 t .... salt
2 T.. lime or lemon juice

• • •

Marinade
½ cup .... yogurt
2 T...finely chopped garlic
2 T.. finely chopped ginger

¼ cup .... finely chopped jalapeno
2 T... tandoori masala
1 t .... red chili powder

• • •

1 cup each ....onion, tomato, & bell pepper slices
1 whole............... lime or lemon cut into wedges
2 whole.................................jalapeno seeded & cut into long strips
1 t .... chaat masala

Method

1. Score the chicken breasts or chicken legs with a knife. Spread the chicken in a tray. Sprinkle with 1 teaspoon salt and 2 tablespoons of lemon juice. Refrigerate for 20 minutes.

2. Combine all the ingredients for the marinade in a blender or a food processor. Transfer marinade to a glass bowl and add chicken, stirring to coat.

3. Cover and refrigerate for at least 6-24 hours.

4. Cooking the chicken: Allow 3-4 extra minutes for bone-in chicken.
   - If using an oven:
   Preheat oven to broil. Arrange the chicken pieces on an oven safe tray in a single layer. Place on the top rack of the oven and bake for 10-15 minutes or until cooked through, turning after 5-7 minutes. Allow it to be charred on the edges.
   - If using barbecue grill:
   Light the grill and leave it on high for direct heat grilling for at least 10-15 minutes.
   Cook the chicken on the grill for 10-15 minutes or until cooked through. It will be charred on edges.

5. Arrange onions, tomatoes, and bell peppers on a serving platter. Add the chicken on top. Garnish with lime or lemon wedges, jalapeno strips, and sprinkle with chaat masala.

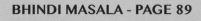

BHINDI MASALA - PAGE 89

CHILI PANEER - PAGE 91

MUTTER PANEER - PAGE 106

STUFFED PEPPERS - PAGE 122

CHAPTER 5: VEGETARIAN MAIN DISHES

Indian vegetarian curries with vegetables and lentils are aromatic, spicy, and very satisfying. Legume and lentil preparations are known as "daal". They are the main source of protein in an Indian vegetarian diet. Tempering or seasoning with different spices make them differ in all the various regions of India. Included in this chapter is a wide selection of vegetarian dishes. Some simple, some complex, but all very pleasing to the palate.

(continued)

Aloo Gobi – North Indian Style

Serves 6
Preparation time: 15 minutes
Cooking time: 20 minutes

Vegan

Vegetarian

Gluten free

Calories 130 • Calories from Fat 70 • Total Fat 7g (Saturated Fat 1g, Trans Fat 0g) • Cholesterol 0mg • Sodium 660mg • Total Carbohydrates 13g (Dietary Fiber 3g, Sugars 3g) • Protein 3g • Provides 40% of daily vitamin C needs

Ingredients

3 T	oil
1 t	cumin seeds
pinch	asafetida/hing
1 t	garam masala
3 T	coriander powder
1 t	turmeric
1 T	ginger
¼ cup	finely chopped jalapeno
1 cup each	onion & potatoes cut into 1" pieces

1 ½ t	salt
2 cups	cauliflower cut into 1" pieces
1 cup	frozen or fresh peas
1 cup	finely chopped tomato

• • •

Garnish

½ cup	finely chopped cilantro
1 whole	lime or lemon cut into wedges

Method

1. Heat 3 tablespoons of oil in a heavy-bottomed pan or wok on medium to high heat. Add cumin seeds and once they turn dark brown, add asafetida/hing, garam masala, coriander powder, and turmeric. Fry the spices for 15 seconds, add ginger and jalapeno, and fry for an additional 30 seconds.

2. Add onion and cook for 1-2 minutes. Add potatoes and ½ the salt and cook for 4-5 minutes. Add cauliflower and the rest of the salt and cook for an additional 4-5 minutes. Add peas and cook for 3-4 minutes. Make sure the potatoes are cooked through. Add chopped tomatoes and mix well.

3. Sprinkle with chopped cilantro and serve with lime or lemon wedges.

4. Serve with chapati (page 48), poori (page 51), or paratha (page 55).

Aloo Gobi – Gujarati Style

Serves 6
Preparation time: 10 minutes
Cooking time: 15 minutes

Vegan

Vegetarian

Gluten free

Calories 120 • Calories from Fat 70 • Total Fat 7g (Saturated Fat 1g, Trans Fat 0g) • Cholesterol 0mg • Sodium 420mg • Total Carbohydrates 11g (Dietary Fiber 3g, Sugars 2g) • Protein 3g • Provides 40% of daily vitamin C needs and 15% of daily vitamin A needs

Ingredients

3 T.. oil
1 t .... cumin seeds
pinch... asafetida/hing
1 cup...................... potatoes cut into ½" pieces
2 cups ....cauliflower cut into ½" pieces
1 cup.................................... frozen or fresh peas

1 t .... salt
1 t .... turmeric
1 T... coriander powder
¼ cup .... finely chopped jalapeno
1 T... lime or lemon juice
¼ cup .... finely chopped cilantro

Method

1 Heat 3 tablespoons of oil in a heavy-bottomed pan or wok on medium to high heat. Add cumin seeds and once they turn dark brown, add a pinch of asafetida/hing, potatoes, and ½ teaspoon salt. Cover and cook potatoes for 3-4 minutes until the edges start turning light brown. Stir occasionally to prevent it from sticking. Add the cauliflower and the rest of the salt and cook for another 4-5 minutes. Add peas and cook for 3-4 minutes.

2 When all vegetables are cooked, add turmeric, coriander powder, jalapeno, lime or lemon juice, and cilantro. Mix well.

3 Serve with chapati (page 48), poori (page 51), or paratha (page 55).

Avial

Vegetarian

Gluten free

Serves 8
Preparation time: 15 minutes
Cooking time: 20 minutes

Calories 140 • Calories from Fat 80 • Total Fat 9g (Saturated Fat 6g, Trans Fat 0g) • Cholesterol 15mg • Sodium 510mg • Total Carbohydrates 13g (Dietary Fiber 3g, Sugars 5g) • Protein 4g

Ingredients

2 T..................................... finely chopped ginger	1 cup... yogurt
¼ cup .... finely chopped jalapeno	½ cup .... sour cream
½ cup .... grated fresh coconut or	• • •
dried unsweetened coconut	2 T.. butter or ghee
½ t... turmeric	1 t .... urad daal
⅛ t...baking soda	½ t .... cumin seeds
1 ½ t.. salt	½ t..mustard seeds
1 cup each ....julienne cut potatoes,	pinch.. asafetida
green beans, carrots, & eggplant	10 leaves................................. limdo/curry leaves
1 cup.. green peas	

Method

1. Combine ginger, jalapeno, and coconut in a food processor to prepare the coconut paste. Set aside.

2. Boil two cups of water in a 4-6 quart pot. Add turmeric, baking soda, and salt. When the water starts to boil, add one vegetable at a time and allow the water to boil in between. Start with potatoes, then add green beans and carrots, and end with eggplant. Cover and cook on medium low heat for 2-3 minutes.

3. Add coconut paste and cook for 2-3 minutes. Add yogurt and sour cream and cook for 1-2 minutes. Remove from the stove.

4. Heat butter or ghee in a small pan. Add urad daal, cumin seeds, and mustard seeds. When cumin seeds turn brown and mustard seeds start to crackle, add asafetida and limdo/curry leaves. Pour it gently over the cooked vegetable mixture.

5. Serve with yogurt rice (page 128) and papadam.

Baigan Bharta

Vegan

Vegetarian

Gluten free

Serves 8
Preparation time: 35 minutes
Cooking time: 30 minutes

Calories 100 • Calories from Fat 70 • Total Fat 7g (Saturated Fat 1g, Trans Fat 0g) • Cholesterol 0mg • Sodium 5mg • Total Carbohydrates 8g (Dietary Fiber 4g, Sugars 2g) • Protein 2g • Provides 30% daily vitamin C needs

Ingredients

2 lb	eggplant	1 cup	finely chopped tomato
¼ cup	oil	2 t	garam masala
1 t	cumin seeds	2 T	coriander powder
1 cup	finely chopped onion	1 t	turmeric
2 T	finely chopped ginger	1 t	red chili powder
2 T	finely chopped garlic		• • •
¼ cup	finely chopped jalapeno	¼ cup	finely chopped cilantro

Method

1 Preheat oven to 450°F. Cut eggplant in half lengthwise and brush with oil on both sides. Roast in the oven for 15 minutes on each side, until soft enough to scoop out. Alternatively, you can grill the eggplant. Allow it to cool for 5-7 minutes in the pan, then remove the eggplant flesh from the skin (discard skin) and finely chop.

2 Heat ¼ cup oil in a heavy-bottomed pot on a medium to high heat. Add cumin seeds, and once they turn dark brown, add the onions and cook for 5-6 minutes until softened. Add ginger, garlic, and jalapeno and cook for 2-3 minutes until fragrant. Add tomatoes and cook for another 3-4 minutes until they start to break down. Add garam masala, coriander powder, turmeric, and red chili powder and cook for 2-3 minutes. Add eggplant and mix. Reduce heat to low, cover, and simmer for 10 minutes. Stir occasionally to prevent sticking.

3 Garnish with cilantro.

4 Serve with chapati (page 48), poori (page 51), or paratha (page 55).

Bhindi Masala

Vegan

Vegetarian

Gluten free

Serves 8
Preparation time: 15 minutes
Cooking time: 30 minutes

Calories 100 • Calories from Fat 60 • Total Fat 7g (Saturated Fat 1g, Trans Fat 0g) • Cholesterol 0mg • Sodium 390mg • Total Carbohydrates 7g (Dietary Fiber 2g, Sugars 2g) • Protein 2g • 40% vitamin C needs

Ingredients

1 lb...okra	1 T.............................finely chopped garlic
¼ cup ....oil	1 t...............................red chili powder
1 t...cumin seeds	1 t.................................garam masala
pinch................................asafetida/hing	1 t...turmeric
1 ½ t...salt	1 cup.............................chopped tomatoes
1 cup.........................thinly sliced onion	• • •
¼ cup ....jalapeno slices – remove seeds	½ cup ....finely chopped cilantro
1 T.................................finely chopped ginger	

Method

NOTE: It is important to wash and dry okra completely before cutting it.

1 Remove top and bottom stems. Depending on the size of okra, cut lengthwise in halves or quarters. Length should be about 2-3".

2 Heat ¼ cup of oil in a heavy-bottomed pan or wok on medium to high heat. Add cumin seeds and once they turn dark brown, add asafetida/hing, okra, and ½ teaspoon salt. Pan fry okra for 4-5 minutes.

3 Remove okra from the oil and set aside.

4 In the remaining oil, add onion and cook for 4-5 minutes. Add jalapeno and cook for 1-2 minutes. Add ginger, garlic, red chili powder, garam masala, and turmeric and cook for 1-2 minutes. Add tomatoes, and rest of salt and cook for 4-5 minutes. Add okra to the mixture and cook for an additional 4-5 minutes.

5 Garnish with cilantro.

6 Serve with chapati (page 48), poori (page 51), or paratha (page 55).

Chana Daal with Cashews

Serves 12
Preparation time: 10 minutes
Cooking time: 20 minutes

Vegan

Vegetarian

Gluten free

Calories 250 • Calories from Fat 125 • Total Fat 14g (Saturated Fat 3, Trans Fat 0g) • Cholesterol 0mg • Sodium 285mg • Total Carbohydrates 24g (Dietary Fiber 6g, Sugars 5g) • Protein 7g

Ingredients

1 cup	chana daal

• • •

2 T	oil
1 t	cumin seeds
2 cups	cashew pieces
¼ cup	raisins
1 cup	diced potatoes
1 cup	finely chopped onion
¼ cup	finely chopped garlic

1 t	turmeric
1 t	red chili powder
2 T	coriander powder
1 t	garam masala
1½ t	salt

• • •

Garnish

1 whole	lime or lemon cut into wedges
2 T	finely chopped cilantro

Method

Note: Instructions for cooking chana daal (page 17).

1. Heat 2 tablespoons of oil in a heavy-bottomed pot on medium to high heat.

2. When oil is heated, add cumin seeds, cashew pieces, and raisins. When cumin seeds turn brown and the raisins begin to puff up, add diced potatoes. Cook for 1-2 minutes, then add chopped onion and garlic and cook for 4-5 more minutes. Add turmeric, red chili powder, coriander powder, garam masala, and salt. Mix well.

3. Add cooked chana daal and water as needed to yield about 6 cups.

4. Bring daal to a boil. Then let it simmer for 5-10 minutes.

5. Garnish with cilantro and lemon wedges.

6. Serve with jeera rice (page 100) or plain basmati rice.

Chili Paneer

Vegetarian

Gluten free

Serves 8
Preparation time: 25 minutes
Cooking time: 20 minutes

Calories 220 • Calories from Fat 130• Total Fat 15g (Saturated Fat 9g, Trans Fat 0g) • Cholesterol 55mg • Sodium 160mg • Total Carbohydrates 7g (Dietary Fiber 1g, Sugars 3g) • Protein 14g • 60% vitamin C, 25% vitamin A, and 30% calcium

Ingredients

¼ cup	oil
1 t	cumin seeds
1 ½ cup	onion cut into 1" pieces
1 cup each	green pepper & red pepper cut into 1" pieces
2 cups	fried paneer cut into 1" pieces (page 19)
1 t	salt
¼ cup each	finely chopped ginger, garlic, & scallion
½ cup	tomato sauce
½ t each	crushed black pepper and red pepper
¼ cup	cashew powder
1 cup	cherry tomatoes
¼ cup	finely chopped cilantro

Method

1. Heat ¼ cup of oil in a heavy-bottomed pan or wok, on medium to high heat. Add cumin seeds and fry until they turn dark brown.

2. Add one vegetable at a time in the following order and cook for 1-2 minutes until completely heated through. First add the onion, cook for 2-3 minutes, then add the red and green peppers and cook for another 2-3 minutes. Add fried paneer and salt and continue stir frying for 2-3 minutes.

3. Add ginger, garlic, scallions, tomato sauce, crushed black pepper, red pepper, and cashew powder. Mix well and cook for 3-4 minutes until fragrant. Stir occasionally to prevent sticking.

4. Add cherry tomatoes and cilantro. Cook for additional 2-3 minutes.

5. Serve with paratha (page 55) or naan (page 53).

Chole

Vegan

Vegetarian

Gluten free

Serves 8
Preparation time: 15 minutes
Cooking time: 40 minutes

Calories 160 • Calories from Fat 70 • Total Fat 8g (Saturated Fat 1g, Trans Fat 0g) • Cholesterol 0mg • Sodium 260mg • Total Carbohydrates 17g (Dietary Fiber 3g, Sugars 3g) • Protein 4g • 20% vitamin C

Ingredients

Gravy

¼ cup	oil
1 t	cumin seeds
4 whole	bay leaves
1 cup	finely chopped onion
¼ cup	finely chopped ginger
¼ cup	finely chopped garlic
6 T	chana masala
1 T	garam masala

1 t	salt
2-10 oz cans/3 cups	cooked whole chickpeas
1 cup	water
1 cup	finely chopped tomatoes

• • •

¼ cup each	finely chopped cilantro, tomatoes, & onions
1 whole	lime or lemon cut into wedges

Method

1 Heat ¼ cup of oil in a heavy-bottomed pot on medium to high heat. Add cumin seeds to the oil and once they turn dark brown, add bay leaves and onion and cook for 5-7 minutes until the onion is soft. Add ginger, garlic, chana masala, garam masala, and salt. Cook for 3-4 minutes until fragrant. Add garbanzo beans, one cup of water, and tomatoes. Bring the mixture to a boil, then lower the heat, cover, and simmer for 20-30 minutes. Stir occasionally to prevent sticking.

2 Garnish with finely chopped cilantro, tomatoes, onions, and lime or lemon wedges.

3 Serve with bhatoora (page 50) or jeera rice (page 100).

Daal Dhokli

Vegan

Vegetarian

Serves 8
Preparation time: 15 minutes
Cooking time: 30 minutes

Calories 280• Calories from Fat140 • Total Fat16g (Saturated Fat 2.5g, Trans Fat 0g) • Cholesterol 0mg • Sodium 390mg • Total Carbohydrates 27g (Dietary Fiber 7g, Sugars 2g) • Protein 9g

Ingredients

Dhokli (dumplings)

1 cup	whole wheat flour
½ t	carom seeds
½ t	salt
½ t	turmeric
½ t	red chili powder
2 T	oil
1/3 cup	water (as needed)

• • •

Daal

½ cup each	split peas & toor daal
2 T	oil

1 t	mustard seeds
1 t	fenugreek seeds
¼ cup	raw peanuts
¼ cup	raw cashews
pinch	asafetida/hing
3 T	coriander powder
1 t each	turmeric, red chili powder, & salt

• • •

Garnish

1 whole	lime or lemon cut into wedges
¼ cup	finely chopped cilantro

Method

NOTE: Instructions for cooking split peas and toor daal (page 17).

1. Mix all the ingredients for the dhokli. Dough should be soft but not sticky. Cover and set aside.

2. Puree daal mixture with an immersion blender and add enough water to yield about 6 cups.

3. Heat 2 tablespoons of oil in a 4 quart pot. Add mustard seeds, fenugreek seeds, and peanuts. When mustard seeds start crackling and fenugreek and peanuts turns brown, add cashews and cook for 1 more minute. Add asafetida/hing, coriander powder, turmeric, and red chili powder, and mix well. Pour the daal mixture slowly and carefully into the pot to avoid splashing hot oil. Add salt. Bring the mixture to a boil, then reduce heat, cover, and simmer for at least 15 minutes. Stir occasionally to prevent sticking.

4. While daal mixture is simmering prepare dhokli as follows:
   - Divide the dough into 6 equal parts and roll each into 8-10" rounds that are the thickness of uncooked tortillas.
   - Cut the dhokli with a pizza cutter into 1" squares. Turn the daal up to medium high. Once it starts boiling, add the dhokli and allow it to boil between adding more dhoklis, stirring to prevent sticking. Cover and let it cook on low heat for 10 minutes.

5. Garnish with cilantro and provide lime or lemon wedges on the side.

6. Serve with ghee (page 18), papadam, and basmati rice.

Daal Dosa

Vegan

Vegetarian

Gluten free

Serves 8
Preparation time: 30 minutes
Cooking time: 30 minutes

Calories 200 • Calories from Fat 70 • Total Fat 7g (Saturated Fat 2.5g, Trans Fat 0g) • Cholesterol 0mg • Sodium 580mg • Total Carbohydrates 25g (Dietary Fiber 7g, Sugars 3g) • Protein 7g • 35% vitamin C and 20% iron

Ingredients

¼ cup each .... moong daal, chana daal, urad daal, & toor daal

½ cup .... basmati rice

• • •

1 t .... crushed red chilies

2 t .... salt

¼ t .... asafetida/hing

2 cups .... finely chopped onion

8-10 pieces .... finely chopped limdo/ curry leaves

¼ cup .... finely grated coconut

¼ cup .... finely chopped jalapeno

¼ cup .... cilantro

• • •

¼ cup .... oil for cooking

Method

NOTE: Rinse and soak all lentils and rice in 4 cups of water overnight or at least 3 hours in lukewarm water.

1. In a food processor or blender, puree the soaked daals and rice, with any leftover water.

2. Add crushed red chilies, salt, asafetida, finely chopped onion, limdo/curry leaves, coconut, jalapeno, and cilantro. Run food processor for another 10 to 15 seconds to allow all the ingredients to mix.

3. Pour the mixture into a bowl. Add additional water if needed to yield about 8 cups of dosa mixture.

4. Heat a 10-12" heavy-bottom pan on medium to high heat. Add ½ teaspoon oil and spread it evenly on the pan. Add 1 cup of batter and spread it with the spatula. The dosa should fill the pan in a thin layer.

5. Cook for 2-3 minutes until the edges start to brown. Drizzle ½ teaspoon oil onto the uncooked side and flip the dosa over with a large spatula. Continue cooking for 2-3 minutes until the edges start turning brown and crispy.

6. Serve with coconut chutney (page 60), sambhar (page 120), and potato vegetables (page 112).

PEAS AND CABBAGE - PAGE 111

CHOLE - PAGE 92

GREEN BEANS - PAGE 99

DAAL DOSA - PAGE 94

Daal Makhani

Vegan

Vegetarian

Gluten free

Serves 8
Preparation time: 20
Cooking time: 45 minutes

Calories 210 • Calories from Fat 90 • Total Fat 10g (Saturated Fat 3g, Trans Fat 0g) • Cholesterol 10mg • Sodium 490mg • Total Carbohydrates 22g (Dietary Fiber 6g, Sugars 2g) • Protein 9g • 15% iron and 15% vitamin C

Ingredients

½ cup each..whole urad, whole lentils/masoor

• • •

4 T..butter or oil
1 t .... cumin seeds
pinch..asafetida/hing
¼ cup each.........................finely chopped ginger, garlic, & jalapeno
3 T.. coriander powder
1 t ....red chili powder

1 t .... turmeric
1 t ....garam masala
1 can ....cooked pinto beans
1 ½ t... salt

• • •

Garnish

1 cup...........................finely chopped tomatoes
½ cup ....finely chopped cilantro
½ cup .... sour cream (optional)

Method

NOTE: Instructions for cooking whole urad and whole lentils (page 17).

1. Heat 4 tablespoons of butter or oil on medium to high heat in a heavy pot. Add cumin seeds, and once they turn dark brown, add asafetida/hing, ginger, garlic, and jalapeno and cook for an additional 1-2 minutes until fragrant. Add coriander powder, red chili powder, turmeric, and garam masala and cook for 1-2 minutes until fragrant. Add cooked lentils, pinto beans, and salt. Add water to yield about 8 cups of lentils. Turn the heat down to low and let it simmer for at least 30 minutes. Stir occasionally to prevent sticking.

2. Transfer daal to a serving bowl and garnish with chopped tomatoes, cilantro, and sour cream.

3. Serve with jeera rice (page 100) or plain basmati rice.

Doodhi Chana Daal

Vegan

Vegetarian

Gluten free

Serves 6
Preparation time: 10 minutes
Cooking time: 20 minutes

Calories 130 • Calories from Fat 25 • Total Fat 3g (Saturated Fat 0g, Trans Fat 0g) • Cholesterol 0mg • Sodium 610mg • Total Carbohydrates 19g (Dietary Fiber 8g, Sugars 2g) • Protein 9g • 20% iron

Ingredients

1 cup...chana daal

• • •

1 T.. oil
1 t ....cumin seeds
2 cups .... doodhi cut into ½" cubes
1 cup...water
⅛ t...baking soda
1 t .... turmeric

1 t ....red chili powder
2 T.. coriander powder
1 ½ t.. salt

• • •

Garnish

1 whole............... lime or lemon cut into wedges
2 T................. finely chopped cilantro for garnish

Method

NOTE: Instructions for cooking chana daal (page 17).

1 Heat 1 tablespoon of oil in a heavy-bottomed pot on medium to high heat. When oil is heated, add cumin seeds and once they turn dark brown, add the doodhi. Add 1 cup of water and baking soda. Cover and cook for 5-7 minutes until tender. Add cooked chana daal, turmeric, red chili powder, coriander powder, and salt. Bring daal mixture to a boil. Add water as needed to yield about 6 cups. Let it simmer for 5-10 minutes. Garnish with cilantro and lemon wedges.

2 Serve with chapati (page 48), poori (page 51), paratha (page 55), jeera rice (page 100), or plain basmati rice.

Fansi Dhokli

Vegan

Vegetarian

Serves 6
Preparation time: 10 minutes
Cooking time: 20 minutes

Calories 120 • Calories from Fat 70 • Total Fat 8g (Saturated Fat 1g, Trans Fat 0g) • Cholesterol 0mg • Sodium 490mg • Total Carbohydrates 13g (Dietary Fiber 3g, Sugars 1g) • Protein 3g

Ingredients

Dhokli (dumplings)

½ cup	whole wheat flour
½ t	carom seeds
⅓ t	salt
½ t	turmeric
½ t	red chili powder
1 T	oil
3-4 T water	approximately

(depending on the quality of flour you may need to adjust the water)

• • •

2 T	oil
1 t	mustard seeds

Pinch	asafetida/hing
1 lb	green beans (fansi) – cut 1/2" long
1 t	salt
⅛ t	baking soda
2 cups	water
1 t	turmeric
1 t	red chili powder
2 T	coriander powder
1 T	lime or lemon juice

• • •

Garnish

¼ cup	finely chopped cilantro

Method

1. Mix all ingredients for the dhokli. Dough should be soft but not sticky. Cover and set aside.

2. Heat 2 tablespoons of oil in a heavy pot on medium to high heat. Add mustard seeds. When seeds start crackling add asafetida/hing, green beans, salt, baking soda and 2 cups of water. Cover and cook on medium heat for 5-7 minutes until beans are tender.

3. While beans are cooking, prepare dhokli as follows:
   - Divide the dough into 3 parts and roll each into 6-8" rounds that are the thickness of uncooked tortillas.
   - Cut the dhokli with a pizza cutter in 1" squares.

4. When beans have finished cooking, add turmeric, red chili powder, coriander powder, and lime or lemon juice. Cover and cook for 2-3 more minutes.

5. Add dhokli to pot and bring to a boil. Cover and let it simmer for 10 minutes.

6. Garnish with cilantro.

7. Serve with chapati (page 48), poori (page 51), or paratha (page 55).

CHAPTER 5
VEGETARIAN MAIN DISHES

Green Beans

Serves 6
Preparation time: 10 minutes
Cooking time: 15 minutes

Vegan

Vegetarian

Gluten free

Calories 70 • Calories from Fat 45 • Total Fat 5g (Saturated Fat 0.5g, Trans Fat 0g) • Cholesterol 0mg • Sodium 410mg • Total Carbohydrates 6g (Dietary Fiber 2g, Sugars 1g) • Protein 1g

Ingredients

2 T	oil
1 t	mustard seeds
1 lb	baby green beans
pinch	asafetida/hing
⅛ t	baking soda
1 t	salt
1 t	turmeric

1 t	red chili powder
3 T	coriander powder
1 T	lime or lemon juice

• • •

Garnish

¼ cup	cilantro

Method

1. Heat 2 tablespoons of oil in a heavy-bottomed pan or wok on medium to high heat. Add mustard seeds. When seeds start crackling add asafetida/hing and green beans, baking soda, and salt and mix well. Cook for 8 to 10 minutes until soft and tender. Stir occasionally to prevent sticking.

2. When the beans are cooked add turmeric, chili powder, coriander powder, lime or lemon juice, and cilantro. Mix well. Cover and cook for 1-2 minutes.

3. Serve with chapati (page 48), poori (page 51), or paratha (page 55).

Jeera Rice

Serves 6
Preparation time: 10 minutes
Cooking time: 20 minutes

Vegan

Vegetarian

Gluten free

Calories 190 • Calories from Fat 70 • Total Fat 8g (Saturated Fat 1g, Trans Fat 0g) • Cholesterol 0mg • Sodium 220mg • Total Carbohydrates 27g (Dietary Fiber 3g, Sugars 2g) • Protein 4g

Ingredients

1 cup	basmati rice

• • •

3 T	butter or oil
1 t	cumin seeds
6 pieces	cloves
3 pieces	cardamom pods

2 pieces	cinnamon sticks
3 pieces	bay leaves
1 cup	onion – cut thin lengthwise
2 cups	water
½ t	salt
1 cup	peas

Method

1. Wash and drain the rice. Set aside for at least 10 minutes.

2. Start boiling 2 cups of water.

3. Heat 3 tablespoons of butter or oil in a heavy-bottomed pot. Add cumin seeds, and once it turns dark brown, add cloves, cardamom pods, cinnamon sticks, bay leaves, and onions and cook for 3-4 minutes until fragrant. Add rice and cook for 5-6 minutes. When the rice starts to turn lightly brown on its edges, add 2 cups of boiling water, salt, and peas. Turn heat down to low. Cover and cook for 20 minutes. Important: DO NOT OPEN THE POT OR STIR THE RICE UNTIL AFTER 20 MINUTES. Fluff it with fork to separate each strand.

Kadhi

Vegetarian

Gluten free

Serves 4
Preparation time: 5 minutes
Cooking time: 15 minutes

Ingredients

1 cup .... yogurt	½ t ....mustard seeds
¼ cup .... besan	½ t .... cumin seeds
4 cups ....water	Pinch.. asafetida
1 t .... salt	¼ t ....red chili powder
1 t .... finely chopped jalapeno	6-8 leaves .... limdo/curry leaves
½ t...grated ginger	
• • •	• • •
	Garnish
2 t .... ghee	1 T................. finely chopped cilantro for garnish
½ t..fenugreek seeds	

Method

1. Combine yogurt, besan, water, salt, jalapeno, and ginger in a pot. Use whisk to smooth the liquid. Bring it to boil on medium low heat. Simmer for 5-10 minutes.

2. In a small pan, combining ghee, fenugreek seeds, mustard seeds, and cumin seeds and cooking on medium low heat. When mustard seeds start crackling and cumin seeds and fenugreek seeds turn brown, add asafetida, red chili powder, and limdo/curry leaves. Pour the mixture on kadhi. Garnish with finely chopped cilantro.

3. Serve with jeera rice (page 100), vegetable pulao (page 127), khichadi (page 103), or plain basmati rice.

JEERA RICE - PAGE 100

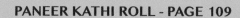

PANEER KATHI ROLL - PAGE 109

MOONG BEANS - PAGE 104

PAVBHAJI - PAGE 110

Khichadi

Vegan

Vegetarian

Gluten free

Serves 6
Preparation time: 15 minutes
Cooking time: 30 minutes

Calories 140 • Calories from Fat 40 • Total Fat 4.5g (Saturated Fat
2.5g, Trans Fat 0g) • Cholesterol 10mg • Sodium 390mg • Total
Carbohydrates 21g (Dietary Fiber 4g, Sugars 1g) • Protein 5g

Ingredients

½ cup	moong daal
½ cup	basmati rice

• • •

2 T	butter, ghee, or oil
½ t	mustard seeds
½ t	fenugreek seeds
pinch	asafetida/hing

10 leaves	limdo/curry leaves
½ cup	thinly sliced onions
1 T	finely chopped ginger
2 T	finely chopped jalapeno
½ t	turmeric
1 t	salt

Method

1. Wash and drain the moong daal and basmati rice together in a bowl. Add 2 ½ cups of water and set the bowl aside.

2. Heat 2 tablespoons of butter, ghee, or oil in a heavy-bottomed pot. Add mustard and fenugreek seeds. When mustard seeds start to crackle and fenugreek seeds turn lightly brown, add asafetida/hing, limdo/curry leaves and onions. Cook for 2-3 minutes. Add ginger and jalapeno and cook for 1-2 minutes until fragrant, then add turmeric and salt. Add the soaked moong daal and rice with the water. Bring to a rolling boil. Reduce heat to low, cover, and simmer for 30 minutes or until all the water is absorbed. Alternatively you can cook it in a pressure cooker or an electric pressure cooker on the same setting as rice.

3. Serve with kadhi (page 101) and papadam.

Moong Beans

Vegan

Vegetarian

Gluten free

Serves 4
Preparation time: 10 minutes
Cooking time: 20 minutes

Calories 130 • Calories from Fat 50 • Total Fat 6g (Saturated Fat 3.5g, Trans Fat 0g) • Cholesterol 15mg • Sodium 580mg • Total Carbohydrates 14g (Dietary Fiber 5g, Sugars 1g) • Protein 6g • 15% iron needs

Ingredients

½ cup .... moong beans	½ t.. turmeric
• • •	1 T........................... coriander powder
2 T.............................. butter or oil	1 t .... salt
½ t.............................. cumin seeds	• • •
pinch.......................... asafetida (hing)	**Garnish**
10 leaves................... limdo/curry leaves	¼ cup .... finely chopped cilantro
1 T..................... finely chopped ginger	1 whole............... lime or lemon cut into wedges
1 T..................... finely chopped jalapeno	

Method

NOTE: Instructions for cooking moong beans (page 20).

1. Heat 2 tablespoons of butter or oil in a heavy-bottomed pot. Add cumin seeds, and once they turn dark brown, add asafetida/hing, limdo/curry leaves, ginger, and jalapeno. Cook for 1-2 minutes until fragrant, then add turmeric and coriander powder and cook for 1-2 minutes. Add cooked moong beans and salt and bring the mixture to a boil. Add water as needed to yield about 4-5 cups of mixture. Cover and simmer for 10-12 minutes. Stir occasionally to prevent sticking.

2. Garnish with cilantro and lime or lemon wedges.

3. Serve with jeera rice (page 100) or plain basmati rice.

Moong Daal

Serves 4
Preparation time: 1 hour
Cooking time: 20 minutes

Vegan

Vegetarian

Gluten free

Calories 160 • Calories from Fat 70 • Total Fat 7g (Saturated Fat 1g, Trans Fat 0g) • Cholesterol 0mg • Sodium 680mg • Total Carbohydrates 17g (Dietary Fiber 6g, Sugars 3g) • Protein 7g • 15% vitamin C and 15% iron

Ingredients

½ cup .... moong daal

• • •

2 T... oil
1 t .... cumin seeds
pinch.. asafetida (hing)
1 cup................................... finely chopped onion
2 T.................................... finely chopped ginger
2 T............................... finely chopped jalapeno

1 cup .... finely chopped tomatoes
1 t .... turmeric
2 T... coriander powder
1 t .... salt

• • •

Garnish

¼ cup .... finely chopped cilantro
1 whole............... lime or lemon cut into wedges

Method

NOTE: Instructions for cooking moong daal (page 17).

1. Heat 2 tablespoons of oil in a heavy-bottomed pot. Add cumin seeds and, once they turn dark brown, add asafetida/hing and onion. Cook for 4-5 minutes until fragrant. Add ginger, jalapeno, and tomatoes and cook for 3-4 more minutes. Add turmeric and coriander powder and cook for 2-3 minutes. Add daal, salt, and bring the mixture to boil. Add water to yield about 4 cups of moong daal mixture. Cover and simmer for 10-12 minutes. Stir occasionally to prevent sticking.

2. Garnish with cilantro and lime or lemon wedges.

3. Serve with jeera rice (page 100) or plain basmati rice.

Mutter Paneer

Vegetarian

Gluten free

Serves 8
Preparation time: 20 minutes
Cooking time: 30 minutes

Calories 290 • Calories from Fat 170 • Total Fat 19g (Saturated Fat 7g, Trans Fat 0g) • Cholesterol 30mg • Sodium 940mg • Total Carbohydrates 20g (Dietary Fiber 5g, Sugars 8g) • Protein 12g • 40% vitamin A, 40% vitamin C, 25% calcium, 15% iron

Ingredients

Gravy

¼ cup	finely chopped jalapeno
¼ cup	finely chopped ginger
1 cup	finely chopped onion
2 T	coriander powder
1 t	garam masala
1 t	turmeric
1 t	red chili powder
½ t	cardamom powder
½ cup	cashew
2 cups	tomato puree

• • •

3 T	oil
1 t	cumin seeds
1 salt	salt
3 cups	peas
2 cups	fried paneer cut into 1/2-inch cubes (page 19)

• • •

½ cup	sour cream
2 T	finely chopped cilantro

Method

1. Puree all the gravy ingredients in a blender. If the mixture is dry, add up to ½ cup water and set aside.

2. Heat 3 tablespoons oil in a heavy-bottomed pot and add cumin seeds. Once they turn dark brown, add the gravy mixture and cook for 6-7 minutes until fragrant. The gravy will be nice and thick. Add peas. Cover and cook for 5-6 minutes on medium heat. Add fried paneer, cover, and cook for 1-2 more minutes.

3. Stir in the sour cream and cilantro just before serving.

4. Serve with chapati (page 48), poori (page 51), or paratha (page 55).

Okra and Potato

Serves 6
Preparation time: 10 minutes
Cooking time: 20 minutes

Vegan

Vegetarian

Gluten free

Calories 140 • Calories from Fat 90 • Total Fat 11g (Saturated Fat 2.5g, Trans Fat 0g) • Cholesterol 0mg • Sodium 590mg • Total Carbohydrates 10g (Dietary Fiber 3g, Sugars 1g) • Protein 2g • 35% vitamin C

Ingredients

¼ cup .... oil

½ t.. cumin seeds

1 cup...........................cut potato into ½" pieces

1½ t.. salt

Note: Add ¼ teaspoon when cooking potatoes and remaining with other spices

1 lb................................. chop okra into ¾" slices

1 t .... turmeric

1 t .... red chili powder

¼ cup .... coriander powder

• • •

Garnish

¼ cup .... finely chopped cilantro

2 T.................... unsweetened shredded coconut

Method

NOTE: It is important to wash and dry okra completely before cutting it.

1 Heat ¼ cup of oil in a heavy-bottomed pan or wok on medium to high heat. Add cumin seeds, and once they turn dark brown, add the potatoes. Sprinkle with ½ teaspoon salt. Cover and cook for 2-3 minutes. Add okra and mix well. Stir fry uncovered for 8 to 10 minutes or until the potatoes and okra is tender. Add rest of salt, turmeric, chili powder, and coriander powder. Mix well and cook for another 2-3 minutes. Remove from heat.

2 Garnish with cilantro and shredded coconut.

3 Serve with chapati (page 48), poori (page 51), or paratha (page 55).

Pahaadi Paneer Kabobs

Serves 12
Preparation time: 20 minutes
Cooking time: 30 minutes

Vegetarian

Gluten free

Calories 170 • Calories from Fat 100 • Total Fat 11g (Saturated Fat 7g, Trans Fat 0g) • Cholesterol 40mg • Sodium 210mg • Total Carbohydrates 8g (Dietary Fiber 1g, Sugars 2g) • Protein 10g • 20% vitamin A, 20% calcium, 40% vitamin C

Ingredients

Marinade

¼ cup each.................. mint, coriander, cashews, yogurt, ginger, & green chilies

2 T.. oil

1 t .... salt

• • •

Cut in 1" cubes for skewers

2 cup.............................. fried paneer (page 19)

1 cup...green bell pepper

1 cup... red bell pepper

1 cup .... cherry tomatoes

1 cup...onion

1 cup...................potatoes sliced to ¼" thickness

• • •

1 cup....................................onion cut into rings

1 whole.............. lime or lemon cut into wedges

2 t ....chaat masala

Method

1. Combine all the ingredients for the marinade in a blender or food processor. Transfer the marinade to a glass bowl, add paneer and vegetables, and stir to coat.

2. Cover and refrigerate for 2-3 hours.

3. Light the grill and leave it on high for direct heat grilling.

4. Thread the paneer into skewers, alternating with green or red bell pepper, cherry tomatoes, onions, and potatoes.

5. Place skewers on the skewer rack on the hottest part of the grill. Cook for 3-4 minutes, turn skewers, apply some marinade with pastry brush, and cook until done. It will be charred on edges.

6. Serve with vegetable pulao (page 127). Arrange vegetable pulao, onion rings, and lime or lemon wedges on a platter. Add skewers on top and sprinkle with chaat masala before serving.

Paneer Kathi Roll

Vegetarian

Serves 8
Preparation time: 20 minutes
Cooking time: 20 minutes

Chapatis:
Calories 150 • Calories from Fat 45 • Total Fat 5g • Cholesterol 0mg • Sodium 75mg • Total Carbohydrates 11g (Dietary Fiber 2g, Sugars 0g) • Protein 2g

Paneer kathi roll stuffing:
Calories 90 • Calories from Fat 60 • Total Fat 7g (Saturated Fat 2.5g, Trans Fat 0g) • Cholesterol 10mg • Sodium 400mg • Total Carbohydrates 3g (Dietary Fiber 1g, Sugars 2g) • Protein 3g • 15% of vitamin A needs, 90% of vitamin C needs

Ingredients

¼ cup .... oil

1 cup each ....onion, red pepper, & green pepper cut into ¼" pieces

1 t .... salt

1 cup.....................................fried paneer cut into ¼" pieces (page 19)

2 T..tandoori masala

1 t ....red chili powder

1 T...lime or lemon juice

• • •

Garnish

1 t ....chaat masala

½ cup .... finely chopped cilantro

Method

NOTE: Instructions for making chapatis (page 48). You can also use regular flour tortillas.

1. Heat 2 tablespoons of oil on medium to high heat in a heavy-bottomed pan or a wok. When oil is heated, first add the onion, cook for 2-3 minutes, then add the red and green peppers and cook for another 2-3 minutes. Stir constantly so the vegetables are stay coated with oil and don't stick to the bottom of the pan. Add salt, fried paneer, tandoori masala, red chili powder, and lime or lemon juice. The mixture should be nice and hot and the vegetables should still be crunchy. Turn off the heat.

2. Heat another flat skillet on medium to high heat. Drizzle some oil and heat chapati or tortilla on both sides. Remove from heat.

3. To eat the kathi roll, spread 1 teaspoon of sweet chutney (page 61) onto a chapati. Add half a cup of the stir fried mixture and sprinkle with chaat masala and cilantro.

4. Fold the chapati at the bottom and wrap both sides over like a burrito.

Pavbhaji

Vegan

Vegetarian

Gluten free

Serves 12
Preparation time: 20 minutes
Cooking time: 40 minutes

Calories 170 • Calories from Fat 90 • Total Fat 10g (Saturated Fat 6g, Trans Fat 0g) • Cholesterol 25mg • Sodium 410mg • Total Carbohydrates 18g (Dietary Fiber 3g, Sugars 3g) • Protein 3g • 15% vitamin A, 50% vitamin C

Ingredients

2 lb... russet potatoes	¼ cup .... finely chopped jalapeno
½ cup ....butter or oil	2 ½ t .... salt
1 cup..................................finely chopped onion	• • •
¼ cup ....finely chopped garlic	¼ cup ....butter for bread (optional)
¼ cup .... pavbhaji masala	¼ cup .... finely chopped cilantro
3 cups ....grated cauliflower	½ cup .... finely chopped tomato
2 cups .... finely chopped tomato	½ cup ....finely chopped onion
1 cup .... peas	1 whole...............lime or lemon cut into wedges

Method

1. Boil 2 lbs of russet potatoes in 6 cups of water for about 20-30 minutes or until cooked. After they finish cooking, run them under cold running water to stop the cooking process. Then peel and coarsely mash with potato masher. This will yield about four cups of coarsely mashed potatoes.

2. Heat ½ cup butter or oil in a heavy-bottomed pan or wok on medium to high heat. Add onion and cook for 7-8 minutes until translucent. Add garlic and cook for 2 more minutes. Add pavbhaji masala and cook for 2-3 minutes until fragrant. Add cauliflower and cook for 5-6 minutes. Add potatoes, tomatoes, peas, jalapeno, salt, and 1 cup of water. Heat it thoroughly. Cover and simmer for 15-20 minutes, stirring occasionally to prevent sticking. After turning off the stove, add cilantro.

3. Serve with soft bread rolls (such as hamburger buns) or croissants. Cut bread in half and apply butter. Grill the bread on heavy-bottomed pan until edges turn brown. To eat, make an open-faced sandwich with approximately ½ cup of pavbhaji on top of the grilled bread.

4. Garnish with ½ tablespoon butter, cilantro, tomatoes, onions, and lime or lemon wedges. Alternatively, you can serve with rice instead of bread.

Peas and Cabbage

Vegan

Vegetarian

Gluten free

Serves 4
Preparation time: 10 minutes
Cooking time: 20 minutes

Calories 140 • Calories from Fat 100 • Total Fat 11g (Saturated Fat 1.5g, Trans Fat 0g) • Cholesterol 0mg • Sodium 620mg • Total Carbohydrates 10g (Dietary Fiber 4g, Sugars 4g) • Protein 3g • 20% vitamin A, 50% vitamin C

Ingredients

3 T.. oil	½ t.. turmeric
½ T...............................mustard seeds	½ t...................................red chili powder
Pinch................................asafetida/hing	1 T.............................. lime or lemon juice
4 cups ....finely chopped cabbage	• • •
1 cup.................................. frozen or fresh peas	3 T...............................finely chopped coriander
1 t .... salt	

Method

1 Heat 3 tablespoon oil in a heavy pan on medium to high heat. Add mustard seeds and once they start to crackle, add asafetida/hing, cabbage, and salt. Stir well. Reduce to medium heat, cover, and cook for 3-4 minutes until cabbage is cooked. Add peas and rest of the spices. Mix well. Cover 2-3 minutes. Garnish with cilantro.

2 Serve with any type of Indian bread.

Potato Vegetables (Dosa Stuffing)

Serves 6
Preparation time: 30 minutes
Cooking time: 20 minutes

Vegan

Vegetarian

Gluten free

Calories 130 • Calories from Fat 60 • Total Fat 7g (Saturated Fat 1g, Trans Fat 0g) • Cholesterol 0mg • Sodium 390mg • Total Carbohydrates 14g (Dietary Fiber 2g, Sugars 2g) • Protein 2g • 35% of vitamin C

Ingredients

1 lb......................................russet potatoes	2 T...sambhar powder
• • •	1 t .... salt
3 T... oil	½ t .... turmeric
1 T...urad daal	¼ cup .... finely chopped jalapeno
1 t ....cumin seeds	2 T.................................... finely chopped ginger
1 t ....mustard seeds	½ cup .... chopped tomato
12 leaves.................neem or limdo/curry leaves	1 T.. lime or lemon juice
⅛ t..asafetida/hing	• • •
1 cup.....................................julienne cut onion	¼ cup .... finely chopped cilantro
2 T.. coriander powder	

Method

1. Boil 1 lb of russet potatoes in 4 cups of water for about 20-30 minutes or until cooked. After they finish cooking, run them under cold running water to stop the cooking process, peel, and cut into ½" pieces.

2. Heat 2 tablespoons of oil in a heavy pan on medium to high heat. Add urad daal, cumin seeds and mustard seeds. When cumin seeds turn brown and mustard seeds crackle, add limdo/curry leaves and asafetida/hing, onion, and cook for 3 to 4 minutes or until the onions are softened. Add coriander powder, sambhar powder, salt, turmeric, jalapeno, and ginger. Add potatoes, tomatoes, and lime or lemon juice and mix well. Lower the heat, cover, and simmer for 7-8 minutes. Stir occasionally to prevent it from sticking.

3. Garnish with cilantro.

4. Serve with daal dosa (page 94), chapati (page 48), poori (page 51), or paratha (page 55).

RAGDO PATTIES (JUST THE PATTIES)

RAGDO PATTIES - PAGE 114

RAWA IDLI - PAGE 117

SAAG PANEER - PAGE 118

Ragdo Patties

Vegan

Vegetarian

Gluten free

This dish makes a complete meal.

Serves 8
Preparation time: 30 minutes
Cooking time: 45 minutes

Calories 240 • Calories from Fat 60 • Total Fat 6g (Saturated Fat.0.5g, Trans Fat 0g) • Cholesterol 0mg • Sodium 870mg • Total Carbohydrates 39g (Dietary Fiber 9g, Sugars 5g) • Protein 8g

Ingredients

Ragdo

1 cup	dried peas (vatana)

• • •

2 T	oil
1 t	cumin seeds
1 cup	finely chopped onion
1 cup	finely chopped tomato
1 ½ t	salt
2 T	coriander powder
1 t	turmeric
1 t	red chili powder

• • •

Potato patties

2 lb	russet potatoes
¾ cup	corn starch (add ½ cup in potatoes and use ¼ cup for applying around patties)
1 t	salt
1 T	lemon juice

• • •

Stuffing for patties

1 cup	coarsely ground frozen or fresh green peas
1 t	oil
1 T	finely chopped jalapeno
¼ t	salt
1 t	lemon juice
½ t	garam masala
¼ cup	finely chopped cilantro

• • •

Garnish

1 T	lime or lemon juice
¼ cup	finely chopped cilantro
½ cup	finely chopped onion

• • •

Approximately 2 cups of oil for frying

Ragdo Patties (continued)

Method

NOTE: Instructions for cooking dried peas (vatana) (page 17).

1. Heat 2 tablespoons of oil in a heavy-bottomed pot on medium to high heat. Add cumin seeds, and one they turn dark brown, add onions and cook for 4-5 minutes until the onions are soft. Add tomatoes and cook for 5-6 minutes until a smooth paste is formed. Add salt, coriander powder, turmeric, and red chili powder. Mix well. Add cooked peas/vatana and water to yield about 6 cups. Cover and simmer for 15 minutes..

2. Boil 2 lb of russet potatoes in 6 cups of water for about 20-30 minutes or until cooked. After they finish cooking, run them under cold running water to stop the cooking process. Then peel and mash well with a potato masher. This will yield about four cups of mashed potatoes.

3. To the mashed potatoes, add ½ cup corn starch, salt, and lemon juice. Mix well and set aside.

4. Coarsely ground peas in a mini food processor. In a small pan on medium heat, add 1 teaspoon of oil. When oil is heated, add coarsely grounded peas and cook for 2-3 minutes on medium heat. Add jalapeno, salt, lime or lemon juice, and garam masala. Cook for 1-2 more minutes. Remove from heat, add cilantro, and set aside.

5. Divide potatoes into 24 parts. Apply a little oil on your fingers and palm. Take 1 part of potato mixture and shape into a 2-3" round, add 1 teaspoon of pea mixture in the middle, then fold the mashed potato over the peas and cover it. Flatten the ball to make a patty. Smooth out edges and lightly coat in corn starch. Arrange potato patties on cookie sheet.

6. Heat oil in frying pan on medium (325°) heat.

7. Fry 6-8 patties at a time for 3-4 minutes or until the color changes to a light golden brown. Move the patties around occasionally to ensure even cooking.

8. For an individual serving, place 3 patties in a bowl. Pour ¾ cup ragdo on top. Garnish with sweet chutney (page 61), cilantro chutney (page 60), onions, and cilantro.

Rawa Dosa

Vegetarian

Serves 8
Preparation time: 10 minutes
Cooking time: 20 minutes

Calories 130 • Calories from Fat 15 • Total Fat 1.5g (Saturated Fat 1g, Trans Fat 0g) • Cholesterol 5mg • Sodium 510mg • Total Carbohydrates 24g (Dietary Fiber 2g, Sugars 2g) • Protein 5g • 25% calcium, 60% iron

Ingredients

1 ½ cups	cream of wheat
½ cup	rice flour
1 cup	buttermilk
1 cup	water
2 t	salt
½ t	baking soda
• • •	
1 T	butter

1 t	urad daal
¼ t	mustard seeds
8-10 leaves	limdo/curry leaves
¼ cup	grated carrot
½ cup	finely chopped peas
¼ cup	finely chopped jalapeno
• • •	
¼ cup	oil

Method

1. Mix cream of wheat, rice flour, buttermilk, water, salt, and baking soda in a bowl.

2. Heat butter in a small pan, then add urad daal and mustard seeds. When urad daal turns light brown and mustard seeds start crackling, add limdo/curry leaves, carrots, peas, and jalapeno. Turn off the heat. Add the mixture to the cream of wheat batter. Set aside for 15-20 minutes.

3. Heat a heavy-bottom pan about 10-12" in diameter on medium heat. Add ½ teaspoon oil and spread it evenly on the pan. Add ½ cup of batter and spread it with the spatula. The dosa should be about 10" to 12" in diameter and slightly thicker than a crepe. Turn heat to high. Cook for 2-3 minutes until the edges start to brown. Drizzle ½ teaspoon oil onto the uncooked side and flip the dosa over with a large spatula. Continue cooking for 2-3 minutes until the edges start turning brown and dosa is crispy.

4. Repeat making dosa until all the batter is gone. Turn heat to medium before you spread the next dosa batter and turn heat back to high while dosa is cooking.

5. Serve with coconut chutney (page 60), sambhar (page 120), and potato vegetables (page 112).

Rawa Idli

Vegetarian

Serves 8
Preparation time: 10 minutes
Cooking time: 20 minutes

Calories 130 • Calories from Fat 15 • Total Fat 1.5g (Saturated Fat 1g, Trans Fat 0g) • Cholesterol 5mg • Sodium 510mg • Total Carbohydrates 24g (Dietary Fiber 2g, Sugars 2g) • Protein 5g • 25% calcium, 60% iron

Ingredients

2 cups	cream of wheat
1 cup	buttermilk
1 cup	water
2 t	salt
½ t	baking soda

• • •

1 T	butter
1 t	urad daal
¼ t	mustard seeds
8-10 leaves	limdo/curry leaves
¼ cup	grated carrot
½ cup	peas
¼ cup	finely chopped jalapeno

Method

1. Mix cream of wheat, buttermilk, water, salt, and baking soda in a bowl.

2. Heat butter in a small pan, then add urad daal and mustard seeds. When urad daal turns light brown and mustard seed starts crackling, add limdo/curry leaves, carrots, peas, and jalapeno. Turn off the heat. Add the mixture to the cream of wheat batter.

3. Boil 2 cups of water in a 6 quart pot for steaming the idlis. Pour 1/3 cup batter into each idli mold and steam for 10-12 minutes. Remove idli molds from pot and cool for 5 minutes. Use a blunt knife to loosen the idlis from the mold.

4. Serve with coconut chutney (page 60) and sambhar (page 120).

Saag Paneer

Vegetarian

Gluten free

Serves 6
Preparation time: 15 minutes
Cooking time: 30 minutes

Calories 230 • Calories from Fat 160 • Total Fat 18g (Saturated Fat 6g, Trans Fat 0g) • Cholesterol 25mg • Sodium 680mg • Total Carbohydrates 13g (Dietary Fiber 4g, Sugars 3g) • Protein 7g • 60% vitamin A, 35% vitamin C, 15% iron, 20% calcium

Ingredients

¼ cup	oil
1 cup	finely chopped onions
¼ cup	finely chopped ginger
¼ cup	finely chopped jalapeno
1 lb	frozen chopped spinach or 8 cups of chopped fresh spinach
⅛ t	baking soda

1 t	salt
½ cup	water

• • •

1 cup	fried paneer – cut into ½" cubes (page 19)
½ cup	sour cream

Method

1. Heat ¼ cup of oil in a heavy-bottomed pot on medium to high heat; add onion and cook for 3-4 minutes until softened. Add ginger and jalapeno and cook for 1-2 minutes until fragrant. Add spinach, baking soda, salt, and ½ cup of water. Mix well. Cover and cook on medium heat for 8-10 minutes, stirring occasionally to prevent sticking.

2. Turn off the heat and let it cool for 10 minutes, then puree using a blender or an immersion blender. Ensure the mixture has sufficiently cooled before pouring into the blender to avoid cracking the glass jar. After pureeing, transfer it back to the pot and bring the mixture to a boil and then add fried paneer, mix well, turn stove off, cover, and set aside for 2-3 minutes.

3. Add ½ cup of sour cream just before serving and mix well.

4. Enjoy with poori (page 51), paratha (page 55), naan (page 53), or plain basmati rice.

Saffron Coconut Rice

Vegan

Vegetarian

Gluten free

Serves 8
Preparation Time: 10 minutes
Cooking Time: 20 minutes

Calories 160 • Calories from Fat 70 • Total Fat 8g (Saturated Fat.6g, Trans Fat 0g) • Cholesterol 10mg • Sodium 290mg • Total Carbohydrates 20g (Dietary Fiber 0g, Sugars 1g) • Protein 2g

Ingredients

1 cup	basmati rice
2 cups	water
½ cup	coconut milk
3 T	butter or oil
6 pieces	cloves

2 small pieces	cinnamon sticks
3 pieces	cardamom pods
1 t	salt
8-10 strands	prepared saffron(page 20)

Method

1 Wash the rice then set aside for 10 minutes to drain.

2 Combine water and coconut milk. Set aside.

3 Heat butter in a pot and add cloves, cinnamon sticks, and cardamom pods. Fry the spices for 1-2 minutes. Add rice, salt, prepared saffron, and coconut milk. When rice starts boiling turn heat to low. Cover it and cook for 20 minutes. DO NOT OPEN OR STIR RICE FOR 20 MINUTES.

4 Enjoy with Chicken Vindaloo (page 73).

Sambhar

Serves 8
Preparation time: 15 minutes
Cooking time: 30 minutes

Vegan

Vegetarian

Gluten free

Ingredients

½ cup ....chana daal	4 T..sambhar powder
½ cup .... toor daal	1 cup.................................. julienne cut eggplant
• • •	1 cup..julienne cut onion
3 T... oil	½ cup .... ½" cut green beans
1 T... urad daal	½ cup .... peas
½ t..mustard seeds	2 T.................... lime or lemon juice or amchoor
½ t.. cumin seeds	1 ½ t.. salt
Pinch.................................. asafetida	• • •
10-12 pieces .... limdo/curry leaves	¼ cup .... finely chopped cilantro

Method

Note: Instructions for cooking chana daal and toor daal (page 17).

1 Puree daal mixture with immersion blender and add enough water to yield about 8 cups. Set aside.

2 Heat oil in a small pan. Add urad daal, cumin, and mustard seeds. When mustard seeds crackle, and the cumin and urad daal turn brown, add the asafetida and limdo/curry leaves. Add sambhar powder and mix well. Add eggplant, onion, green beans, and green peas and cook for 3-4 minutes.

3 Pour pureed daal mixture in the pot and bring it to boil. Add lime/lemon juice/amchoor and salt and bring it to boil.

4 Cover and simmer for 20-25 minutes.

5 Serve with rawa idli (page 117), rawa dosa (page 116), or masala wada (page 33).

Spinach & Eggplant

Vegan

Vegetarian

Gluten free

Serves 6
Preparation time: 10 minutes
Cooking time: 15 minutes

Calories 90 • Calories from Fat 60 • Total Fat 7g (Saturated Fat 1g, Trans Fat 0g) • Cholesterol 0mg • Sodium 470mg • Total Carbohydrates 6g (Dietary Fiber 3g, Sugars 2g) • Protein 1g • 30% vitamin A, 25% vitamin C

Ingredients

3 T... oil	1 t .... salt
¼ t..................................fenugreek seeds	2 cups .... eggplant cut into 1" cubes
1 lb.......................... frozen chopped spinach or 8 cups of fresh chopped spinach	1 cup............................. finely chopped tomato
¾ cup ....water	1/4 cup .... finely chopped jalapeno
1/8 t................................baking soda	2 T.. coriander powder
	1 t .... turmeric

Method

1. Heat 3 tablespoons of oil in a heavy-bottomed pot on medium to high heat. When oil is heated, add fenugreek seeds. When fenugreek turns dark brown, add spinach, ¾ cup water, baking soda, and salt. Mix well.

2. Add eggplant, tomato, jalapeno, coriander powder, and turmeric. Do not mix. Cover and cook on medium heat for at least 6-7 minutes.

3. After the eggplant has softened and cooked, mix well.

4. Serve with chapati (page 48), poori (page 51), or paratha (page 55).

Stuffed Peppers

Serves 4
Preparation time: 20 minutes
Cooking time: 30 minutes

Vegan

Vegetarian

Gluten free

Calories 260 • Calories from Fat 170• Total Fat 18g (Saturated Fat 5g, Trans Fat 0g) • Cholesterol 0mg • Sodium 160mg • Total Carbohydrates 18g (Dietary Fiber 7g, Sugars 8g) • Protein 10g • 90% vitamin A, 80% vitamin C

Ingredients

16 whole .... small red, yellow, & orange sweet peppers

• • •

Stuffing

2 T .... oil

1 t .... salt (use ½ t in stuffing and ½ t in sprinkling over pepper)

1 cup ....coarsely ground peanuts

¼ cup .... unsweetened grated coconut

2 cups .... finely chopped cilantro

¼ cup .... coriander powder

1 t ....garam masala

1 t .... turmeric

1 t .... red chili powder

2 T.. lime or lemon juice

• • •

3 T... oil

1 t .... cumin seeds

1 t ....mustard seeds

½ t .... salt

Method

1. Remove the top of each pepper with a knife and remove all the seeds.

2. Combine all the ingredients for the stuffing in a bowl, using only ½ teaspoon of salt. Divide mixture into 16 equal parts. Stuff each pepper and set aside in a bowl. When all the peppers are stuffed, sprinkle ½ teaspoon of salt and gently toss them in a bowl.

3. Heat 2 tablespoons of oil in a heavy-bottomed pan or wok on medium to high heat. Add mustard and cumin seeds. When mustard seeds crackle and cumin seeds turns brown, add the stuffed peppers to the pan, laying them on their sides. Turn heat to medium low and cover. Cook for 5-7 minutes on each side. To check if the peppers are done, insert a knife into one side. If it goes through easily, the pepper is cooked. Cook for additional time if the peppers are not soft enough.

4. Serve with chapati (page 48), poori (page 51), or paratha (page 55).

Upama

Vegetarian

Serves 6
Preparation time: 10 minutes
Cooking time: 25 minutes

This dish makes a great breakfast.

Calories 200 • Calories from Fat 70 • Total Fat 8g (Saturated Fat 5g, Trans Fat 0g) • Cholesterol 20mg • Sodium 610mg • Total Carbohydrates 27g (Dietary Fiber 2g, Sugars 3g) • Protein 5g

Ingredients

4 T	butter
1 t	urad daal
½ t	cumin
½ t	mustard seeds
Pinch	asafetida
10 leaves	limdo/curry leaves
1 cup	finely chopped onion
1 cup	cream of wheat

1 cup	yogurt
2 cups	boiling water
½ t	salt
2 T	finely chopped ginger
2 T	finely chopped jalapeno

• • •

¼ cup	finely chopped cilantro
2 T	finely chopped onion
2 T	finely chopped tomato

Method

1. Heat 4 tablespoons of butter in a nonstick pot on a medium heat. Add urad daal, cumin, and mustard seeds. When urad daal and cumin turn brown and mustard seeds start to crackle, add asafetida, curry leaves, and chopped onion. Cook for 3-4 minutes. Add cream of wheat. Turn heat to medium low and cook cream of wheat until it turns light brown, stirring constantly for about 6-7 minutes.

2. Add yogurt, 2 cups of boiling water, salt, ginger, and jalapeno. Mix well. Cook for 3-4 minutes on medium low heat, stirring constantly. Cover and simmer for 3-4 minutes.

3. Transfer to a bowl. Garnish with cilantro, onion, and tomato.

4. Serve with coconut chutney (page 60).

Vegetable Biryani

Vegetarian

Gluten free

Serves 12
Preparation time: 45 minutes
Cooking time: 1 hour

Calories 370 • Calories from Fat 190 • Total Fat 21g (Saturated Fat 7g, Trans Fat 0g) • Cholesterol 25mg • Sodium 550mg • Total Carbohydrates 37g (Dietary Fiber 3g, Sugars 6g) • Protein 9g • 40% vitamin A, 35% vitamin C, 15% calcium

This is one of my favorite recipes so, although the list of ingredients and process can seem overwhelming, I encourage you to give it a try, as it is absolutely worth the effort and time. I've given instructions in steps that you can follow, one at a time, setting different preparations aside so that you can put them all together at the end. As with all recipes, read through it carefully before you begin and assemble all the ingredients. A good biryani is a pleasure to behold and eat! Make extra (this recipe serves 12) and enjoy it the next day.

Ingredients - Part 1

½ cup .... oil	2 cups .... basmati rice
2 cups .... caramelized onions (page 18)	15-20 strands........................... saffron + 2 T milk

Method - Part 1

1. Caramelizing of the onion gives the gravy a rich flavor and brown color. Keep ¼ cup of caramelized onion aside for garnish, use the rest in the biryani paste.

2. Wash and drain rice, then soak in 4 cups of water.

3. Prepare saffron (page 20).

Ingredients - Part 2

5 T..biryani masala	5 pieces .... bay leaves
¼ cup each............ finely chopped garlic & ginger	10 pieces .... cloves
• • •	2 cups each .... potatoes & tomatoes
¼ cup each....................... sliced almonds, raisins,	cut into big pieces
& cashew pieces	1 t .... salt
• • •	½ cup .... yogurt

Method - Part 2

1. Combine in a blender or food processor biryani masala, garlic, ginger, caramelized onion, and ½ cup of water to make a biryani paste. Keep paste aside.

2. Heat ½ cup of oil in a 6 quart heavy-bottomed pot, add almonds and cashews, and cook until edges turn brown, then set aside.

3. Add raisins and cook until they puff up, then set those aside as well.

Vegetable Biryani (continued)

Ingredients - Part 3

5 pieces .... bay leaves	1 t .... salt
2 cups ....potato cut into 2" pieces	2 cups .... fried paneer (page 19)
1 cup each .... green beans, carrots, &	
cauliflower cut into 1" pieces	

Method - Part 3

1 In the remaining oil, add bay leaves, cloves, and biryani paste and cook for 3-4 minutes on medium heat.

2 Add potatoes, green beans, carrots, cauliflower, and 1 teaspoon of salt and mix well. Cover and cook on low heat for 5-7 minutes, stirring occasionally to allow even cooking. Cover and simmer for an additional 10 minutes.

3 Add paneer and mix well. Set aside.

Ingredients - Part 4

2 t .... salt	½ cup .... milk
¼ cup .... butter	¼ cup each............ finely chopped cilantro & mint
¼ cup .... lime or lemon juice	¼ cup each.............................caramelized onion

Method - Part 4

PREHEAT OVEN TO 350°F

1 Boil 4 cups of water. Drain the soaked rice and add it to the boiling water. Add 2 teaspoons of salt and boil for 5-6 minutes uncovered. Drain any remaining water from the rice.

2 Add rice on top of vegetables and paneer and do not stir or mix. Cut ¼ cup of butter into small pieces and dot the top of the rice. Drizzle ¼ cup lime or lemon juice on top of the rice. Add ¼ cup of milk to saffron mixture and drizzle on top of the rice. Drizzle an additional ¼ cup of milk over the top of the rice. DO NOT STIR.

3 Cover the pot with aluminum foil and place the lid on top. Bake in the oven for 30 minutes.

4 After removing the biryani from the oven, add cilantro, mint, and caramelized onion. Toss gently and transfer it to a serving dish. Decorate with almonds, cashews, and raisins.

5 Serve with yogurt or cucumber raita (page 62) and papadam.

DAAL MAKHANI - PAGE 96

VEGETABLE BIRYANI - PAGE 124

YOGURT RICE - PAGE 128

KADHI - PAGE 101

Vegetable Pulao

Vegan

Vegetarian

Gluten free

Serves 6
Preparation time: 10 minutes
Cooking time: 40 minutes

Calories 240 • Calories from Fat 90 • Total Fat 10g (Saturated Fat 4.5g, Trans Fat 0g) • Cholesterol 15mg • Sodium 610mg • Total Carbohydrates 36g (Dietary Fiber 4g, Sugars 8g) • Protein 5g • 45% vitamin A, 25% vitamin C

Ingredients

1 cup .... basmati rice	2 cups .... boiling water
• • •	1½ t... salt
3 T .... butter, ghee or oil	½ cup .... peas
¼ cup .... golden raisins	½ cup .... green beans cut into ½" pieces
¼ cup ....cashews	½ cup .... finely diced carrot
½ t.. cumin seeds	1 t...garam masala
6 whole .... cloves	½ t... turmeric
3 whole................................... cardamom pods	¼ cup .... finely chopped jalapeno
2 pieces .... 2" long cinnamon sticks	1 T.. lemon juice
4 pieces .... bay leaves	• • •
1 cup .... thinly sliced onions	¼ cup .... finely chopped cilantro

Method

1. Wash and drain basmati rice. Set aside for at least 10 minutes.

2. Heat 3 tablespoons of butter, ghee, or oil in a heavy-bottomed pot on medium to high heat. Add raisins until they puff up, then remove from heat and set aside. Add cashews, cook for 2 minutes or until edges turn slightly pink, and set aside.

3. In the same butter, ghee,or oil, add cumin seeds. Once they turn dark brown, add cloves, cardamom, cinnamon, and bay leaves and cook for 1 minute. Add the onions and cook for 4-5 minutes until the onions are softened. Add rice and continue to cook until the rice starts to turn slightly pink, about 5-6 minutes. Add 2 cups of boiling water. Add salt, peas, green beans, carrots, garam masala, turmeric, finely chopped jalapeno, and lemon juice. Reduce the heat to low, cover, and cook for 20 minutes.

4. Transfer the cooked pulao to a bowl or platter. Garnish with the raisin, cashews, and cilantro.

5. Enjoy with yogurt, cucumber raita (page 62), or kadhi (page 101) and papadam.

Yogurt Rice

Vegetarian

Gluten free

Serves 8
Preparation time: 10 minutes
Cooking time: 35 minutes

Calories 150 • Calories from Fat 25 • Total Fat 3g (Saturated Fat 0.5g, Trans Fat 0g) • Cholesterol 5mg • Sodium 450mg • Total Carbohydrates 28g (Dietary Fiber 2g, Sugars 7g) • Protein 7g • 30% vitamin A, 20% vitamin C, 15% calcium

Ingredients

1 cup	basmati rice
3 cups	water
• • •	
1 T	ghee or oil
2 T	urad daal
1 t	cumin seeds
1 t	mustard seeds
1/8 t	asafetida/hing
4 to 6 leaves	limdo/curry leaves

1 ½ t	salt
3 cups	yogurt
1 cup	milk
½ cup	finely chopped cucumber
¼ cup	finely chopped ginger
¼ cup	finely chopped jalapeno
½ cup	grated carrot
¼ cup	finely chopped cilantro

Method

1. Wash and drain the rice. Add 3 cups of water, and bring to a boil. Cover and cook on low heat for 25 minutes until all the water is absorbed.

2. Heat 1 tablespoon of ghee or oil in a heavy-bottom pot. Add urad daal, cumin seeds, and mustard seeds. When mustard seeds start to crackle and the cumin seeds turn brown, add asafetida/hing and limdo/curry leaves. Turn heat to medium. Add cooked rice, salt, yogurt, milk, cucumber, ginger, jalapeno, grated carrot, and cilantro. Mix well. Cook on low to medium heat for 4-5 minutes.

3. Transfer to a bowl.

4. Serve immediately or chill in the refrigerator and serve cold.

128

CHAPTER 5
VEGETARIAN MAIN DISHES

GULAB JAMOON - PAGE 136

RASAGULLA - PAGE 142

GOLPAPDI - PAGE 135

COCONUT BURFI - PAGE 133

CHAPTER 6: DESSERT

Indian desserts are always tempting and mouth watering - they complete the meal. You can have hot desserts in the winter and cold desserts in the summer. They are rich with use of butter or ghee, sugar, nuts, whole grain, fruits, and spices like cardamom, nutmeg, and saffron. Some take a long time to make and others can be made in 10-15 minutes. Lassi is perfect to go with any spicy meal.

Carrot Halwa

Vegetarian

Gluten free

Serves 8
Preparation time: 15 minutes
Cooking time: 45 minutes

Calories 360 • Calories from Fat 150 • Total Fat 17g (Saturated Fat 8g, Trans Fat 0g) • Cholesterol 35mg • Sodium 90mg • Total Carbohydrates 51g (Dietary Fiber 4g, Sugars 45g) • Protein 4g • 380% of vitamin A

Ingredients

½ cup ....butter or ghee (page 18)	1 ½ cup .... sugar
8 cups ....shredded carrots	1 t .... cardamom powder
1 cup.. whole milk	½ cup .... ground almond & pistachio

Method

1. In a heavy-bottomed pan, heat butter or ghee. Once melted, add shredded carrot. Cook on medium heat for 8-10 minutes until the liquid is gone.

2. Add milk and continue cooking for 10-15 minutes, stirring frequently until the mixture thickens. Check to see if carrots are completely cooked. If not, continue cooking until they are.

3. Add sugar and continue stirring for at least 10-12 minutes on medium heat, until the halwa starts to clump together and ghee starts to separate. Add cardamom and nuts and remove from the stove.

4. Serve hot by itself or with a scoop of vanilla ice cream. Alternatively, refrigerate for at least 2-3 hours and serve cold.

132

CHAPTER 6
DESSERTS

Coconut Burfi

Serves 8
Preparation Time: 10 minutes
Cooking Time: 20 minutes

Vegetarian

Gluten free

Calories 160 • Calories from Fat 70 • Total Fat 8g (Saturated Fat.5g, Trans Fat 0g) • Cholesterol 10mg • Sodium 0mg • Total Carbohydrates 22g (Dietary Fiber 1g, Sugars 20g) • Protein 1g

Ingredients

¾ cup .... sugar

¼ cup .... water

1 cup .... unsweetened finely grated coconut

¼ cup .... chopped cashew

2 T................................. butter or ghee (page 18)

½ t.. cardamom powder

Method

1. Grease pie plate with butter and set aside.

2. In a heavy pan on low to medium heat, combine water and sugar. Stir continuously so sugar dissolves and the syrup starts thickening. Cook for 3-4 minutes. Place one to two drops on a small plate. Allow it to cool a little. When you rub the drop between your thumb and index finger and it forms a single string, then the syrup is ready.

3. Add coconut and stir until bubbles start forming at the edge of the pan. Add butter or ghee and mix well, before adding cashews and cardamom powder. It will be done cooking when the mixture thickens and does not stick to the pan.

4. Transfer mixture to the buttered dish and spread evenly. Cut into pieces while mixture is still warm.

5. Let it cool completely before transferring to a serving tray.

Date Rolls

Vegan

Vegetarian

Gluten free

Serves 16
Preparation time: 20 minutes
No cooking required

Calories 210 • Calories from Fat 130 • Total Fat 14g (Saturated Fat 2g, Trans Fat 0g) • Cholesterol 0mg • Sodium 10mg • Total Carbohydrates 20g (Dietary Fiber 3g, Sugars 14g) • Protein 5g

Ingredients

3 cups .... pitted dates – preferable medjool or any variety of soft dates

1 t ....melted butter or oil

1 cup each ....chopped walnut, almond, & cashew

2 T...poppy seeds

Method

1. Place the dates in a glass bowl and microwave for one minute at a time for up to 3 minutes until they are hot and soft. Grease the bowl of the stand mixer and add the dates. Use the dough hook to make a paste, then add the nuts and continue mixing until it forms a ball.

2. Divide the mixture into four parts and roll into logs about 1-1½" in diameter. Put the rolls in an airtight container and refrigerate for 4-6 hours.

3. Place poppy seeds in a plate, roll logs in poppy seeds, cut the log into 1/2" slices with a sharp knife.

4. Store the rolls in an airtight container.

Golpapdi

Vegetarian

Serves 8
Preparation time: 10 minutes
Cooking time: 20 minutes

Calories 210 • Calories from Fat 110 • Total Fat 12g (Saturated Fat 7g, Trans Fat 0g) • Cholesterol 30mg • Sodium 0mg • Total Carbohydrates 23g (Dietary Fiber 2g, Sugars 12g) • Protein 2g

Ingredients

½ cup .... butter or ghee (page 18)
1 cup .... whole wheat flour
¾ cup .... grated jaggery
¼ t .... cardamom powder
¼ cup .... milk (as needed)

• • •

1 t .... poppy seeds
1 T each .... coarsely ground pistachios & almonds

Method

1. Melt butter or ghee in a heavy pan on low to medium heat. When melted, add the whole wheat flour and cook for 8-10 minutes until it turns dark brown and looks grainy.

2. Remove from heat and add the jaggery and cardamom powder. If the mixture is crumbly, add 3-4 tablespoons of milk. Stir well so the jaggery is completely melted and the milk is mixed in. Transfer to a pie dish. Sprinkle with the poppy seeds, coarsely ground almonds, and pistachios. Press it down with a pastry roller. Cut into 16 pieces while it is still warm with a pizza cutter or knife.

3. Let it cool, then store in an airtight container.

Gulab Jamoon

Vegetarian

Serves 12
Preparation time: 20 minutes
Cooking time: 45 minutes

Calories 180 • Calories from Fat 45• Total Fat 5g (Saturated Fat 3g, Trans Fat 0g) • Cholesterol 20mg • Sodium 120mg • Total Carbohydrates 33g (Dietary Fiber 2g, Sugars 27g) • Protein 2g

Ingredients

½ cup ....heavy cream
½ cup ....cream of wheat
½ cup .... Carnation milk powder
¼ T ....baking soda

• • •

Syrup

1 ½ ....cup sugar
3 cup...water
½ T .... cardamom powder
⅛ t..saffron

• • •

Approximately 2 cups of oil for frying

Method

1. Combine heavy cream and cream of wheat in a glass bowl and refrigerate overnight in an airtight container for at least 6-8 hours.

2. Combine sugar, water, cardamom, and saffron in a pot. Bring the liquid to boil and let it simmer for 10-15 minutes.

3. While syrup is simmering, transfer the cream and cream of wheat mixture to a food processor. Add the milk powder and baking soda. Knead for 3-4 minutes until the dough is very smooth, the divide into 24 parts. Grease your hands and roll each piece into a smooth ball.

4. Heat the oil in a frying pan on low to medium heat. When temperature reaches between 300° to 325°F, fry 8-10 pieces at a time on low heat, stirring often to brown evenly all sides. Drain on paper towels.

5. Allow syrup to cool for about 10 minutes. Add jamoon to the syrup to let it soak. The gulab jamoon will get softer and slightly lighter in color.

6. Serving suggestions: If serving hot, serve right away, otherwise, microwave for 1 minute if serving later. If serving cold, refrigerate for 4-6 hours.

Kheer

Vegetarian

Gluten free

Serves 12
Preparation Time: 10 minutes
Cooking Time: 45 minutes

Calories 220 • Calories from Fat 35• Total Fat 4g (Saturated Fat 1.5g, Trans Fat 0g) • Cholesterol 15mg • Sodium 130mg • Total Carbohydrates 36g (Dietary Fiber 1g, Sugars 29g) • Protein 10g

Ingredients

12 cups .... whole or 2% fat milk	¼ cup each.................... finely chopped almonds & pistachio
½ cup .... uncooked rice	
1 cup.. sugar	15-20 strands............ prepared saffron (page 20)
½ t.................................... cardamom powder	

Method

1. Grease 6-8 quart heavy pan with butter or ghee. Add 12 cups of milk and uncooked rice and bring to boil on medium to high heat. Stir occasionally to prevent sticking. Boil until the milk has reduced to about one half its original volume, approximately 15-20 minutes.

2. Add sugar, cardamom, almonds, and pistachios and stir well, then add the saffron.

3. Serve hot or chilled.

Mango Lassi

Vegetarian

Gluten free

Perfect drink for a hot summer day.

Serves 8
Preparation time: 10 minutes
No cooking required

Calories 160 • Calories from Fat 10 • Total Fat 1g (Saturated Fat 0.5g, Trans Fat 0g) • Cholesterol 5mg • Sodium 45mg • Total Carbohydrates 36g (Dietary Fiber 1g, Sugars 35g) • Protein 4g

Ingredients

2 cups .... mango peeled and sliced or canned pureed mango	2 cups .... crushed ice
2 cups .... yogurt	1 cup... sugar
4 cups .... water	1 t ....rose water
	¼ t... salt

Method

1. In a blender combine the mangoes, yogurt, water, crushed ice, sugar, rose water, and salt. Blend until smooth.

2. Pour in a glass and enjoy with spicy Indian meal.

Kaju Katri

Vegetarian

Gluten free

Serves 24
Preparation time: 15 minutes
Cooking time: 15 minutes

Calories 250• Calories from Fat 140• Total Fat 16g (Saturated Fat 3g, Trans Fat 0g) • Cholesterol 0mg • Sodium 5mg • Total Carbohydrates 24g (Dietary Fiber 1g, Sugars 14g) • Protein 5g

Ingredients

4 cups ....cashew powder

1 ½ cup .... sugar

¼ cup .... milk

6 pieces .... edible silver foil (optional)

¼ t... butter

Method

1. Butter a half sheet cookie tray and set aside.

2. Combine sugar and milk in a frying pan on very low heat. Stir the mixture until all the sugar is dissolved. Add cashew powder and stir continuously for at least 4-5 minutes until it forms a cohesive ball and does not stick to the pan. If the mixture is crumbly, add 1 to 2 tablespoons of milk. Once smooth, transfer to the prepared cookie sheet. Using a pastry roller, spread the mixture to an even thickness.

3. Immediately apply silver foil while still warm. With a pizza cutter, slice into 1" strips, cut diagonally to form diamond-shaped pieces. Let it cool for 30 minutes.

4. Store in an airtight container.

Moong Daal Sheera

Vegetarian

Gluten free

Serves 12
Preparation time: 15 minutes
Cooking Time: 1 hours and 30 minutes

Calories 260 • Calories from Fat 120• Total Fat 13g (Saturated Fat 8g, Trans Fat 0g) • Cholesterol 30mg • Sodium 15mg • Total Carbohydrates 33g (Dietary Fiber 4g, Sugars 23g) • Protein 5g

Ingredients

1 cup .... moong daal

¾ cup .... butter or ghee (page 18)

1 cup .... whole milk

1 ¼ cup .... sugar

10-15 strands .... prepared saffron (page 20)

• • •

t .... cardamom powder

2 T each ....coarsely ground pistachios & almonds

Method

1 NOTE: Wash and soak moong daal in lukewarm water for at least 3-4 hours.

2 Drain the moong daal and coarsely grind it in food processor. Set aside.

3 Heat ghee in a heavy bottomed pan on medium low heat. Add coarsely ground moong daal and cook for 10-12 minutes. When the mixture is heated through and bubbling, turn heat to low and cook for 40-45 minutes until it becomes golden brown in color. Stir constantly to prevent sticking.

4 Add 1 cup of warm milk and 1 cup of warm water. Cook for 10-15 minutes until the liquid is completely absorbed and ghee starts to separate.

5 Add sugar and mix well. Cover and simmer for 15-20 minutes or until ghee separates. Stir occasionally to prevent sticking.

6 Add the saffron mixture and cardamom powder and mix well. Turn stove off.

7 Garnish with almonds and pistachios. Serve hot.

Poranpoli

Vegan

Vegetarian

Serves 8
Preparation time: 20 minutes
Cooking time: 40 minutes

Calories 380 • Calories from Fat 110• Total Fat 12g (Saturated Fat 4.5g, Trans Fat 0g) • Cholesterol 15mg • Sodium 5mg • Total Carbohydrates 61g (Dietary Fiber 7g, Sugars 26g) • Protein 10g • 15% of daily iron needs

Ingredients

½ cup each......................chana daal & toor daal

12-15 strands............ prepared saffron (page 20)

• • •

2 cups ....whole wheat flour

2 T.. oil

1 cup......................................water (as needed)

• • •

1 cup.. sugar or jaggery

¼ cup ....ground almonds

1 t ....cardamom

½ t.. nutmeg powder

• • •

4 T.................................butter or ghee (page 18)

Method

NOTE: Instructions for cooking chana daal and toor daal (page 17).

1. Combine wheat flour, oil and water and prepare dough that is soft but not sticky. Cover and set aside for 30 minutes.

2. Drain any extra water remaining after the daals have been cooked, then puree with an immersion blender or whisk. Transfer pureed daal to a heavy pot. Cook on medium heat for 5-7 minutes until it becomes like soft dough, stirring constantly to prevent sticking. Add sugar or jaggery, turn heat to medium, and cook for another 3-4 minutes, stirring constantly to prevent splattering. If it starts splattering, remove from heat, mix well, and return back to heat. Add almonds, cardamom, nutmeg, 2 tablespoons of butter or ghee, and saffron mixture. The mixture should be soft like dough and it will thicken as it cools down.

3. Set aside and let it cool completely. This mixture is called "Poran". "Poli" means round bread. Hence it is called Poranpoli.

4. Divide dough and Poran in 16 equal parts. Heat a griddle on medium flame.

5. Form balls with each piece of dough and roll them in a plate of flour to coat. Sprinkle flour on a clean work surface and roll into 6-8" in rounds with a rolling pin. Place one part poran mixture in center of dough. Gather the dough on edges and fold over the stuffing. Pinch extra dough and seal it. Sprinkle flour and gently pat it, placing gathered side face down. Gently roll it back out to a 6" round.

6. Transfer the poranpoli to the griddle and cook it on both sides until it starts showing bubbles and some brown spots.

7. Transfer poranpoli to a plate and apply butter or ghee generously on top.

MOONG DAAL SHEERA - PAGE 139

CARROT HALWA - PAGE 132

RASAMALAI - PAGE 143

PORANPOLI - PAGE 140

Rasagulla

Vegetarian

Gluten free

Calories 240 • Calories from Fat 45• Total Fat 5g (Saturated Fat 2.5g, Trans Fat 0g) • Cholesterol 15mg • Sodium 55mg • Total Carbohydrates 45g (Dietary Fiber 0g, Sugars 44g) • Protein 5g • 15% of calcium needs

Ingredients

1 cup...paneer (page 19)
3 cups ....water
1 ½ cup .... sugar
¼ t... cardamom powder

• • •

2 T.............................coarsely chopped pistachio
2 T...rose water

Method

1. Knead paneer to make smooth pliable dough for at least 3-4 minutes. Make 25 to 30 mini balls and keep aside.

2. In a heavy, wide bottomed pan add water, sugar, and cardamom powder and stir on high heat until sugar dissolves completely. When the syrup starts boiling, add the paneer balls and simmer for 3-4 minutes before reducing the heat to medium. Using a spoon or spatula, move the paneer ball to the center of the pan, they will tend to migrate to the edges as the syrup boils. Cover and cook for 10-12 minutes. Open the lid every 3-4 minutes to let the vapor release. Remove from the stove once the balls have about doubled in size.

3. Let cool completely. Transfer to a serving bowl and garnish with chopped pistachios and rose water.

Rasamalai

Vegetarian

Gluten free

Serves 8
Cooking time: 30 minutes

Calories 210 • Calories from Fat 45• Total Fat 5g (Saturated Fat 2.5g, Trans Fat 0g) • Cholesterol 20mg • Sodium 120mg • Total Carbohydrates 34g (Dietary Fiber 0g, Sugars 32g) • Protein 9g

Ingredients

Basoondi (Gravy)

6 cups .... milk

½ cup ....condensed milk

½ cup .... sugar

6-8 strands...saffron

½ t... cardamom powder

• • •

¼ cup .... finely chopped nuts – pistachio, almond and cashew

Method

NOTE: Prepare Rasagulla (page 142) and saffron (page 20).

1. Grease a 6-8 quart heavy pan with butter or ghee, then add milk and bring it to boil on medium to high heat. Boil until the milk has reduced to about one half of its original volume.

3. Add condensed milk, sugar, saffron, and cardamom powder.

4. Remove rasagulla from syrup and arrange in a flat serving dish, pour warm basoondi mixture on top. Garnish with finely chopped nuts.

5. Refrigerate for 3 to 4 hours before serving.

Seviyan

Vegetarian

Serves 12
Preparation time: 10 minutes
Cooking time: 30 minutes

Calories 170 • Calories from Fat 45• Total Fat 5g (Saturated Fat 2g, Trans Fat 0g) • Cholesterol 10mg • Sodium 75mg • Total Carbohydrates 26g (Dietary Fiber 1g, Sugars 21g) • Protein 7g • 20% daily calcium needs

Ingredients

1 T .... butter or ghee (page 18)	¼ cup .... raisins
6 cup .... milk	½ cup .... condensed milk
½ cup .... seviyan	½ cup .... sugar
¼ cup .... slivered almonds	½ t .... cardamom powder
¼ cup .... whole pistachios	¼ t .... strands of saffron

Method

1. Grease heavy pan with butter or ghee, then add 6 cups of milk. Bring the milk to boil on medium to high heat, and allow it to simmer while you are preparing the seviyan.

2. Prepare saffron (page 20).

3. Heat 1 tablespoon of butter or ghee in a small pan. When melted, add seviyan, almonds, pistachios, and raisins. Cook for 2-3 minutes until seviyan is lightly browned and the raisins start to puff up. Transfer it to the boiling milk. Simmer the mixture on low to medium heat for about 10 minutes. Then, add condensed milk, sugar, cardamom, and saffron, and boil on medium heat for 4-5 minutes.

4. This can be served hot in the winter or cold in the summer. To serve cold, refrigerate for at least 3-4 hours.

Sheera

Vegetarian

Serves 8
Preparation Time: 10 minutes
Cooking Time: 25 minutes

Calories 290 • Calories from Fat 80• Total Fat 8g (Saturated Fat 4g, Trans Fat 0g) • Cholesterol 20mg • Sodium 230mg • Total Carbohydrates 49g (Dietary Fiber 1g, Sugars 32g) • Protein 5g

Ingredients

11-12 strands .... prepared saffron (page 20)	1 cup .... sugar
¼ cup .... butter or ghee (page 18)	1 t .... cardamom
2 cups .... milk	• • •
¼ cup .... raisin	¼ cup .... coarsely ground almond
1 cup .... cream of wheat	

Method

1. Grease 4 quart heavy pan with ½ teaspoon of butter or ghee and add the milk. Bring it to a boil on medium to high heat. Stir occasionally to prevent sticking. Let milk simmer while preparing the cream of wheat mixture.

2. Melt remaining butter or ghee in a heavy pan on medium low heat. Add raisins and cook for 1 minute or until they begin to puff up. Add cream of wheat and cook for 5-6 minutes until light and fluffy. Stir constantly to prevent burning and sticking. Carefully add hot milk and stir for 3-4 minutes. Add sugar and cook for another 2-3 minutes or until the ghee starts to separate. Add saffron and cardamom and mix well. Cover and simmer for 2-3 minutes.

3. Transfer in a bowl and garnish with almonds. Serve hot.

Shrikhand

Vegetarian

Gluten free

Serves 12
Preparation Time: 30 Minutes
No cooking required

Calories 170 • Calories from Fat 25• Total Fat 3g (Saturated Fat 1g, Trans Fat 0g) • Cholesterol 5mg • Sodium 40mg • Total Carbohydrates 30g (Dietary Fiber 0g, Sugars 30g) • Protein 7g

Ingredients

12-15 strands .... prepared saffron (page 20)

3 cups .... plain Greek yogurt

½ cup .... milk powder

1 ½ ....cup sugar

½ t...cardamom

½ t.. nutmeg

• • •

¼ cup .... coarsely ground almonds & pistachios

Method

1. In a bowl, combine the Greek yogurt, milk powder, sugar, cardamom, and nutmeg. Set aside for 15-20 minutes. This will allow the sugar to melt and all the ingredients to release their flavors. Add saffron and stir again. Mix well.

2. Transfer to a serving bowl. Garnish with almonds and pistachios. Refrigerate for at least 6-8 hours before serving.

INDEX

Made in the USA
Charleston, SC
16 June 2016